Praise for *Ezra: Unleashing the Power of Praise*

"Living a life of praise changes us—the hard becomes holy, and the ugly transforms into beauty. In this study of Ezra, Carol Tetzlaff walks us through ancient text, leading us to practical real-life application. An excellent study encouraging us to believe God for the rebuilding of every broken place in our lives."

—Debbie Alsdorf
Author of *Deeper*, *The Faith Dare*, and *It's Momplicated*

"What a timely read! In a season of political, social, and interpersonal tumult, the wisdom of this seven-week study serves as invaluable and practical encouragement. Carol Tetzlaff has an incredible gift of navigating a rarely studied, oft-overlooked book of the Bible and pointing readers to the hope found only in the worship of God through candor, relatable stories, and wisdom. This study, *Ezra: Unleashing the Power of Praise*, would be perfect for small groups, women's gatherings of all sorts, worship teams, and for anyone needing a reminder of the love of God and the transformative power of surrender in worship."

—Amberly Neese
Comedian, author, speaker
Author of *The Belonging Project: Finding Your Tribe and Learning to Thrive*

"Exile. What an unusual subject from which to build a case for experiencing, developing, and practicing worship! Except . . . it's the human context within which God asks us to do that very thing. So when you think of real-life worship, what better Bible book to work from than one focused on exile and restoration? One like *Ezra*. And your guide, Carol Tetzlaff, is remarkably equipped to unfold the patterns and outcomes of a worship-fed life journey. Wherever you are on that journey, Carol will take the 'know, be, do' practiced by Ezra, apply it to worship, and through it, help you set your worship compass to take you through exile into the eternal presence of God."

—Dr. Bert Downs
Chancellor, Western Seminary

"Carol is a worship leader who understands that God wants more than our singing when it comes to worship. *Ezra: Unleashing the Power of Praise* is a great Bible study that integrates biblical history, personal stories, great discussion questions, and personal reflection opportunities. I could go on and on, but frankly my biggest endorsement is that I will be purchasing the study for all the worship teams across our campuses at Palm Valley Church!"

—Ryan Nunez
Lead pastor of Palm Valley Church, Goodyear, AZ

"Carol unwraps God's Word to help us rediscover the meaning of worship. This is a timely study that guides us to align our hearts toward proper worship so we can develop a daily walk of obedience. The words—Rediscover, Realize, Recognize, Reclaim, and Reflect—will take on new meaning as they guide you to life transformation. Get your highlighter ready for an adventure into the Word!"

—VICKI VOYCE
Director of LIFT AZ (Leaders in Fellowship Together)

"Have you been in a season of drought, disappointment, or discouragement? Friend, you are not alone. This world's flash and shine holds no healing for the child of God, but His Word surely does. With the heart of a worshiper and the skill of a Bible teacher, Carol Tetzlaff guides us through a rich study of Ezra, a powerful and hidden gem meant for seasons just like this. I could not put my highlighter down. I found revival in these pages, the cure for listless and lifeless worship. And so will you. I promise."

—LEE NIENHUIS
Author, international Bible teacher,
host of the Moms in Prayer podcast

rebuilding broken into beautiful through worship

a 7-week Bible study

Ezra

Unleashing the Power of Praise

CAROL TETZLAFF

REDEMPTION
PRESS

Published by Redemption Press, PO Box 427, Enumclaw, WA 98022.

Toll-Free (844) 2REDEEM (273-3336)

Redemption Press is honored to present this title in partnership with the author. The views expressed or implied in this work are those of the author. Redemption Press provides our imprint seal representing design excellence, creative content, and high quality production.

ISBN 13: B&W soft: 978-1-64645-230-9
Color: 978-1-64645-461-7
ePub: 978-1-64645-231-6
Mobi: 978-1-64645-232-3

Library of Congress Catalog Card Number: 2020925713

This book is dedicated to the one who took
my "once upon a time" and made it "happily ever after."
My adoring husband, who encouraged me to take
that first brave step and begin my publishing journey.
My heart is so in love with you, Kelley Tetzlaff!

And to the One who is the Author of my salvation.
Jesus!
May the story of my life be found as worship in Your eyes.
All for Your glory!
Oh, how I love You!

Foreword

Never enough. That's the mantra of our culture. We strain toward new, more, better, and best. Living in meagerness and dissatisfaction despite our abundance. We seek to fill ourselves with things that seep through our flesh, yet leave our souls empty.

Ezra: Unleashing the Power of Praise points us on a path toward fullness. We learn the secret behind our wants and how to find our fill of God's goodness yet again. We learn how to worship. And how to cease worshiping the wrong things that leave us forever wanting more, while receiving less and less satisfaction.

Let's follow the people of Israel onto a new path of promise. A life rebuilt. Focus restored. Satisfaction regained. Offer before God all of our broken pieces, shattered through the endless pursuit of pleasure and purpose apart from Him. Find life anew, full of hope and power, as we discover a life of worship as God designed it to be.

Through this journey through Ezra, we realize that right before us awaits abundance immeasurable and all that our souls crave.

Let's unleash the power of praise in our lives and discover the full and purposeful lives we've always wanted, yet always had. This study will help us uncover how to live in it, no longer being dragged down in dissatisfaction by the false substitutes of our culture. We will learn to rebuild our lives on a foundation that steadies us, guards us, and guides us to the glorious life God intended.

ERICA WIGGENHORN

Bible teacher and author of *Unexplainable Jesus: Rediscovering the God You Thought You Knew*

CONTENTS

Welcome to *Ezra: Unleashing the Power of Praise*

We can unleash the power of praise in our everyday lives as we engage in the work to rebuild a life of worship. This worship is not defined in a corporate setting of our local church gathering, but it is found in the common places of our lives. It is the praise of our souls that weaves its way through the very fabric of our days, whether at the kitchen sink or at the boardroom table. Our lives expound the praises of our King as everything within us exclaims the words of Psalm 145:

> I will extol you, my God and King,
> > and bless your name forever and ever.
> Every day I will bless you
> > and praise your name forever and ever.
> Great is the Lord, and greatly to be praised,
> > and his greatness is unsearchable. (Psalm 145:1–3)

Here are a few items that will assist you in making the most of your study:

- The main text used for this study is the English Standard Version of the Bible. Occasionally the text will be from a different Bible version, which will be noted.
- The study is seven weeks long. Each week contains five days of assignments.
- This study will have greater impact in your life if you set up a regular time each day to complete the written assignments. Engaging daily will set a pattern in your life for personal worship.
- Begin your time of study with prayer. Ask the Holy Spirit to use the words of the Scripture along with those written in this study book to teach you. The questions are designed to bring understanding of the text and application to your life. Do not be constrained by the black-and-white text on the page. Allow the Spirit to

use what you are reading to guide you to a deeper understanding of the truths He has for you to discover.

- At the end of each day of study, you will be invited to a personal reflection that corresponds to the application from the text through the section entitled "Unleash the Power of Praise." Each day of the week will follow a pattern that will become familiar to you through your time in this study.

    Day One: Rediscover the meaning of worship.

    Day Two: Realize the challenges found in the misalignment of our worship.

    Day Three: Recognize the truths found in God's Word that encourage worship.

    Day Four: Reclaim the blessings of God found as we worship Him alone.

    Day Five: Reflect on what God is teaching us personally about our worship.

- At the end of each week of study, there are questions taken directly from the study for use in a group setting, as well as additional questions for discussion.
- Dedicated notes pages are included within the study for each week.
- Video teaching is available at caroltetzlaff.com.
- A teaching outline and commentary is provided at caroltetzlaff.com and can be used by a group leader or a Bible study teacher to add a live teaching element to your group time.
- This study is based on the Word of God and requires the participant to utilize the text each day. A list of all the Scriptures for each day of study is provided for quick access at caroltetzlaff.com.

I would love to hear from you during your time in this study. You can contact me several ways:

- Website: www.caroltetzlaff.com
- Facebook: Carol Tetzlaff - Author
- Instagram: Carol_Tetzlaff

Thank you for joining me in this study as we unleash the power of praise in our everyday lives through the rebuilding of our worship. I would consider it an honor to pray for you during your time in the book of Ezra. Please connect with me so I can encourage you through prayer: CarolLynnTetzlaff@gmail.com.

Recall

An Introduction to Ezra

INTRODUCTION

So, whether you eat or drink, or whatever you do, do all to the glory of God.

1 CORINTHIANS 10:31

I find myself in the same place several times each day—standing at the kitchen sink. Several years ago, I complained aloud at my Bible study, "How can two people dirty so many dishes?" An older, much wiser friend spoke these words to me: "Dear one, doing dishes reminds us of God's provision in our life. You have food to make and a precious family to serve. Instead of groaning over the task, utter words of gratefulness from a heart of worship."

Those words have replayed in my mind so many times while in the kitchen throughout the years. Can the simple act of doing dishes become worship? I have discovered the answer to be yes! In fact, everything we do is worship!

No, seriously, it is!

If it is not God who resides at the center of our everyday worship, something else will take His place.

Why? Because God created us to be worshipers.

I am so excited to explore the book of Ezra with you by rebuilding broken to beautiful through worship.

We will begin by briefly looking back at the deterioration of worship found within God's people, which caused them to be taken captive by their enemy. This led them to a place of complete dependence on God as He eventually returned them to their home to rebuild their temple and restore their worship.

Oftentimes when we hear the word *worship*, we immediately think of singing or a service we attend at church. For many years I equated the term *worship* with that thirty-minute time slot during the Sunday morning church service when we would pull out hymnals and sing. Worship to me was music.

I'm sure I am not the only one who has thought this. When a church has a worship leader, worship songs, and a worship band, it only seems logical to assume worship has to do with singing.

Although God's intent of worship remains unchanged, I have been brought into a more correct definition over the past few decades as I consider His declaration of worship, and maybe you have as well.

Worship, in its simplest sense, can be summed up by the words of Paul in Romans 12:1: "Present your bodies as a living sacrifice, holy and acceptable to God, which is your spiritual worship."

So there you have it. According to this verse, worship is you and me placing our lives on the altar of surrender and submitting to God and to His perfect will. The next verse goes on to tell us this is done by the transformation of our minds—a continual process that changes us from the inside out. The theological term for this is *sanctification.*

The word *sanctification* means to set apart for a specific use. For the believer, it is a process that takes place in our everyday living. It is the setting apart of our actions and attitudes from who we once were to who we are becoming for the purpose of being used by God in His service. Sanctification results in godly living and culminates in our glorification when we meet our Savior face to face.

Although this act of worship may sound simple enough, the reality is it takes complete dependence on the Holy Spirit as He guides us to surrender in every single aspect of our lives.

You see, we were created to worship. All of creation was designed to do this. We read in Psalm 19 that even the stars above worship, for "the heavens declare the glory of God."

The problem in worship occurs when we choose the wrong object to which to bend our knee. You may be thinking you don't need to worry about that, because you probably don't have golden statues displayed in your home that you pray to for help. But the objects of our worship are much more powerful than statues. The things we worship can have overwhelming control over us, and we don't even realize it. The things we worship take up our time and use up our resources in the place of the almighty God.

The people found in the narrative of the Old Testament faced the same issues with their worship. They chose to worship gods of foreign nations, which resulted in the turning of their hearts away from the one true God. This moved them toward a life of complete disobedience and disregard for what He had commanded of them as His chosen people.

They found themselves taken captive by foreign nations, and their means of worship—the very temple that housed God's presence—was not only far away from them, but was completely destroyed.

And this is what brings us to our journey through the book of Ezra—a journey that began in the hearts of a rebellious people who were given a severe punishment, a hopeful promise, and miraculous permission to bring them to a place of rebuilding the very foundation of their worship.

Through this historical account of the ancient, coupled with the reality of our present, we will be invited to unleash the power of praise as we:

- Rediscover the meaning of worship.
- Realize the challenges found in the misalignment of our worship of God.
- Recognize the truth found in God's Word that encourages us to worship.
- Reclaim the blessings of God found as we worship Him alone.
- Reflect on what God is teaching us personally about our worship.

We will also take a moment each week to develop the habit of worship at the kitchen sink. This is a call to practicing His presence in the ordinary, everyday tasks of our lives. As we become more aware of living a life of proper worship, we allow God to turn the mundane minutes into miraculous moments as our hearts are drawn toward Him.

It may seem a bit uncomfortable at first, but soon this practice will become a habit. We may even see it trickle into the lives of those in our family as we encourage a life that is constantly aware of our attitude of worship.

There is so much to learn during our time together over the next seven weeks. I'm so glad you have chosen to join me as we rebuild broken to beautiful through worship. No matter where you are today, I am praying God will use this time in His Word to move all of us toward Him as we become women who fully surrender ourselves on His altar of our everyday worship!

Defining Worship

In order to get the most from our study, let's take a few moments and define *worship*.

When do you typically hear the word *worship* used?

What words, thoughts, or actions come to your mind when you think about worship?

What do the following verses tell us about worship?

      1 Samuel 15:22

      Isaiah 29:13

      Romans 12:1–2

Write a brief statement from these verses defining God's idea of worship.

How does this idea contrast or complement the idea of worship from your thoughts above?

Your picture of worship may be enhanced or even challenged through this study. There is much to learn about ourselves and our God as we engage in the daily practice of unleashing the power of praise.

Take a moment and ask God to teach you through this time in His Word. Ask Him to speak to your heart, to your needs, and to your specific struggles in the daily routines of life. It will be thrilling to look back in the end and see what He

has done while unleashing the power of praise through worship for your good and His glory!

REVIEW AND DISCUSSION

This portion of the study can be used in two ways.

If you are doing this study solo, you can take the time to answer the questions as a review to what you have experienced in the previous week.

If you are doing this study in a group, these questions will lend to group discussion.

1. If you are doing this study in a group, take a few minutes this first week of study and allow each person to introduce themselves.

2. What comes to mind when you hear the word *worship*?

3. Since most people equate worship with a gathering of God's people, recall one of the most memorable worship experiences you've attended. What is it that made it so unforgettable?

4. After reading through the introduction, what are you most looking forward to within the next seven weeks of study?

5. What are your greatest challenges when you engage in a weekly study that requires daily assignments?

6. If you are doing this study in a group, how can you offer encouragement to those in your group? If you are doing this study alone, how can you find encouragement to continue the work that is required in Bible study?

7. Pray for one another as you embark on this journey together.

TEACHING NOTES

_____

_____

_____

_____

_____

_____

_____

_____

_____

_____

_____

_____

_____

_____

_____

_____

_____

_____

_____

_____

_____

_____

Remember

Week One

WEEK ONE • DAY ONE

When I was a little girl, I begged my mom for a piano. I vividly remember the day when my wish came true as I was told a surprise was arriving at our home. A knock was heard at the door, and I was instructed to hide in the kitchen while something big and grand was being delivered. I wondered what it could it be, as the struggle happening on the other side of the kitchen sounded like an elephant was being delivered and placed in the center of the living room. After what seemed like forever to a five-year-old, the sound of the tinkling piano keys brought me bursting around the corner into the living room to find my dreams were now a reality. There it sat in all its glory—the dark cherrywood casing, the shiny black and white keys, and a wooden bench that would become my throne for many years to come.

Years of lessons and hours upon hours of practicing would follow, even into my college years. It wasn't quite as glorious as I had dreamed it would be; in fact, it was downright hard work. But looking back, I'm thankful for the persistence of my mother and grandmother who did everything necessary, including forcing me at times to practice, to bring to my intellect a musical language that became as natural as saying the ABCs.

This gift of music brought me to a place where I am now leading the worship team at my church. Through this ministry, I realize more than ever that musical talent is secondary to the alignment of the individual's heart toward God in our worship.

During this first week, we will take the time to grasp a biblical concept of worship. This will be accomplished as we look into the story of some familiar accounts in Scripture. The idea of worship began in the heart of God to be displayed through the response of His people. We will also review the history of the exiles we will be introduced to in the book of Ezra. There is great value found in knowing their story, as we engage in the transformation that will take place within these men and women in our narrative.

When the heart of our worship to God is displaced, the result can be detrimental, not only to ourselves, but also to the people around us. This is true today, just as it was in the very beginning. When God created man, He created us to worship, and the focus of that worship was Him! You may recall what happened as the serpent crept into the garden telling Adam and Eve the lie that instead of worshiping God, they could become just like Him. This lie is still believed today, for we live in a world that appears to have the same dilemma as the early church in Rome.

» **What does Romans 1:25 state about the direction of worship?**

» **What was the result of their wrong worship from Romans 1:28, 32?**

Worship that is placed in something other than God is sin. To be honest, that something most often begins with a *who* and points back to us. When we place our desires, our ambitions, and our thoughts contrary to God's, our heart is displaced and our actions reflect this misalignment.

» **Look at the account from Genesis of Cain and Abel. Read Genesis 4:2–8.**

» **What offerings did Cain and Abel bring before the Lord?**

» **How did the Lord receive each of their offerings?**

» **What was Cain's reaction to God's response toward his offering?**

» **What was God's warning toward Cain's behavior?**

» **What happened as a result of Cain allowing sin to rule over him?**

» **What does Hebrews 11:4 reveal about the acceptance of Abel's offering?**

Both Cain and Abel offered sacrifices of worship to God. The acceptance was not found in the quality of the offering, but in the condition of their heart. It was Abel's faith that set him apart. He was a righteous man according to other accounts that recall his offering (Matthew 23:35; 1 John 3:12).

God is so much more concerned about the alignment of our hearts than what our hands can produce or our mouths can express. He wants us, you and me, to give ourselves over to His will and to His way. Even the smallest offering of worship can become much when given to Him with complete surrender.

The truth of God looking deep within our hearts is shown in the Old Testament account of choosing David as the heir to the throne, along with the New Testament account of the widow's offering.

At the beginning of the monarchy in Israel, the appointment of Saul as king had resulted in disappointment. In this next passage we find Samuel on his way to Bethlehem, having been sent by God to anoint a new king over Israel. Read the account in 1 Samuel 16:6–13.

Samuel had a very different idea than God about who should be king. What factors did Samuel take into account?

» **What was God looking for in the next king of Israel?**

In the New Testament, we find a very different scenario with the same truths to learn.

Read the account in Mark 12:41–44 as Jesus teaches His disciples from this exchange in the temple.

Once again, man has a different idea than Jesus as to what is best. Compare and contrast the following:

» **Who are the two types of people in this account?**

» **What did each give?**

» **From what did they give?**

» **Express a truth you can surmise from these two accounts.**

» **Can you recall an example when you gave preferential treatment to someone because of their outward appearance or actions? State it below, as well as what you experienced or learned from the outcome.**

Unleash the Power of Praise:

Rediscover the meaning of worship.

First Samuel 16:7 gives us this truth: "For the Lord sees not as man sees: man looks on the outward appearance, but the Lord looks on the heart."

What does this verse reveal about the way God sees us?

Which is easier for us to accept: the way man sees us on the outside or the way God sees us on the inside? Why?

Think about your everyday interaction with people. It could be with your family, your coworkers, your church family, or just the people you meet in your everyday life. If you were to take an inventory of what these people see in your actions and hear in your words, what are the three things they would observe?

Now do the hard work. Using those same observations, what is it that God would reveal within the motivations of your heart in these actions and words? If you are unsure, take a moment and pause to ask Him. He often speaks the loudest when we are quiet before Him.

Use the space below to record your thoughts as you apply 1 Samuel 16:7 to the

observations of your own life. This can be done through words, phrases, drawings, symbols, song, or any other means of expression as an act of worship to God.

For the Lord sees not as man sees: man looks on the outward appearance,
but the Lord looks on the heart.

1 SAMUEL 16:7

WEEK ONE • DAY TWO

We ended Day One looking at the danger of outward preferential treatment. To be honest, I have been guilty of this very thing on more than one occasion—meeting someone new, passing a quick judgment, and then months or even years later getting to know them and realizing I had missed out on some precious years of friendship. Oh, that we would be women who would pray to see people as God sees them, recognizing the beauty found within their soul rather than the judgment we declare in silence over their appearance and actions.

On the other hand, I have experienced the appearance of godliness through eloquent speech and sacrificial actions only to find that what laid deep within their heart was betrayal and deceit. I assure you that these actions lead to a path of destruction like a bulldozer destroying everything in its way. Jeremiah speaks truth as he writes, "The heart is deceitful above all things, and desperately wicked: who can know it?" (Jeremiah 17:9 KJV).

I'll tell you who knows it—God! We can't hide anything from Him. It doesn't matter how gussied up we get on the outside; He sees the deepest, darkest places within the secret parts of our lives. But do you know what is completely glorious about this all-knowing God? If we allow Him the space, He will expose the darkness within our hearts and lead our outward actions to display His light. It's certainly not easy, but it is worth it.

The exiles we will join in this study received a word from God during one of the darkest times in their lives. Their sin was exposed, which led them into captivity. Just when things couldn't get much worse, they got some very good news from Ezekiel.

» **What promises did they receive through Ezekiel from God in Ezekiel 36:24–28?**

» **verse 24**

» **verse 25**

» **verse 26**

» **verse 27**

» **verse 28**

God is indeed in the business of making things new, and this includes us—praise His name! When we allow ourselves to become overwhelmed with this truth and give God access to every corner of our life, our worship is brought into proper vertical alignment with Him. This alignment brings us a life of joy only the Lord can offer, as we embrace that He is indeed our strength.

There is a truth that is not found in the book of Psalms, even though it sounds like something that would gush from the pen of the poet. The verse, "The joy of the Lord is your strength," actually comes from Nehemiah 8:10. The context is found within the narrative of the life of the exiles of Judah as Ezra reads them the law. And do you know what gives them joy as they hear the law read to them? They understand it.

Their understanding brought rejoicing, which led them into repentance and ushered them into a life steered by proper worship. And that's exactly where this study will lead us— into a place where we experience joy no matter our circumstances. Rejoicing is always evident in a life surrendered.

This life of worship is not lived in our own strength. Look at Romans 8:9–11. Fill in the blanks for the following verses using the ESV (English Standard Version) Bible.

You, however, are not in the flesh but in the _____, if in fact the

_____ of God dwells in you. . . . But if Christ is in you, although the body is dead because of sin, the _____ is _____ because of righteousness. If the _____ of him who raised Jesus from the dead _____ _____ _____, he who raised Christ Jesus from the dead will also give _____ to your mortal bodies through his _____ who dwells in _____.

Look at verse 11 again.

Who raised Jesus from the dead? _____

Who lives in you? _____

It is the Spirit who gives us victory! It is the Spirit who gives us life, my friend! We don't have to do this on our own, and in fact, we can't even if we try. As we navigate this life of proper worship, we have the Holy Spirit within us to help prompt our heart to practice His presence every single moment. Inviting God to have access into even the most insignificant areas of our lives will create an environment of worship that focuses on Him alone.

Unleash the Power of Praise:

Realize the challenges found in the misalignment of our worship of God.

Each day you will find an opportunity to unleash the power of praise that guides you through a practice that will eventually become a permanent pattern of daily life. These moments will lead you to align your heart in proper worship.

Take a moment and think about a task you find mundane that must be done this week. Write down only one task below.

As you complete that task in the next few days, be aware of what you are thinking about, your attitude, and even your emotions. Record your discovery below:

Day one:

Day two:

Day three:

We will revisit this later.

This is the time where we stop and reflect, giving thanks to the One who is going to empower us to live a life of worship. It is God alone who is our strength, and He will give us joy on this journey as we align our heart to His.

Write your words of reflection in the space below.

An authentic life is the most personal form of worship.
Everyday life has become my prayer.
—Sᴀʀᴀʜ Bᴀɴ Bʀᴇᴀᴛʜɴᴀᴄʜ

WEEK ONE • DAY THREE

As the book of Ezra opens, the people return to a land that has been destroyed by the enemy. As their eyes behold the destruction of their city, they are reminded of the events in the past that led to their demise. And as they stumble through the rubble wondering how rebuilding could even be possible, they may have thought back to the past events that brought their city to its knees.

Many of the exiles who returned to rebuild would have been very young at the time of the destruction, and most of them would have been born in captivity in a foreign land. This very fact offers the beauty that is found within their story. Parents and grandparents alike would have been the ones to retell stories of the past, instilling within the next generation the hope of a future that could be claimed.

The stories told did not bode well for God's people. They recalled their blatant disregard for the one true God and all He had promised them if they would keep their worship directed toward Him alone. Failure to follow after God had destroyed not only their relationship with Him, but also the very place where the presence of God resided—the temple.

Before we get too deep into the story, let's take a look back at the fall of Jerusalem toward the end of its demise in the book of 2 Kings. I hope you will enjoy this brief lesson on the history of Judah.

Josiah

Josiah became king when he was just eight years old. We are told in 2 Kings 22 that he was a leader who followed after the heart of God. Throughout his reign he repaired the temple, followed the book of the law, and restored the Passover, although at the end of his life he chose to take things into his own hands. Fearful that Egypt would partner with the Assyrians to wage war against Babylon, Josiah made a grave mistake in attacking Egypt. Ironically, it would not be the Assyrians they would need to worry about, but the Babylonians.

This event cost Josiah his life, for he was killed in the battle. Taken back to the city and buried in his tomb, possibly no one mourned his death more than Jeremiah the prophet. This man of God knew the demise that awaited God's people. Sure enough, just twenty-three years after Josiah's death, the city would fall to the Babylonians, and all of Jeremiah's words of judgment would come to pass.

Johoahaz (Shallum)

Due to the defeat Judah experienced against Egypt, their independence was lost as Josiah's youngest son took the throne after his father's death. He reigned only three months before Egypt took Johoahaz into exile, as predicted by Jeremiah.

Read Jeremiah 22:10–12 and state the prophet's instruction to Judah and the outcome of Shallum's exile.

Jehoiakim (Eliakim)

With the Egyptian pharaoh overseeing the affairs in Judah, he placed Eliakim, another son of Josiah, on the throne and changed his name to Jehoiakim.

The prophet Jeremiah received a word from the Lord to write a letter to the king warning him of the disaster to come.

> » **What was the hopeful outcome if the king received the warning from this letter, according to Jeremiah 36:3?**

A servant of Jeremiah, Baruch, delivered the message from the Lord to the people of Judah. As those in the king's court were made aware of these words, they became afraid and took the letter to show the king, while at the same time warning Baruch and Jeremiah to hide.

> » **What was the response of the king when he received the warning from this letter in Jeremiah 36:23–25?**

Once again, the reigning king disregarded the warnings of destruction and the plea to return to true worship, resulting in his fall. King Jehoiakim would come to find that his alliance with Egypt would be worthless, as Babylon not only began a three-year siege against Judah, making them servants, but also took all that belonged to Egypt.

After a few years of reprieve from Babylon and a decision from the king to not pay the taxes due to them, the king was bound and taken as prisoner before being killed (2 Chronicles 36:5–6 and 2 Kings 24:6).

Jehoiachin

Another king took the throne for a short three months. Jehoiachin would lead the royal family and the leaders in Jerusalem to surrender to Babylon.

In Jeremiah 20:5, a warning was given to the people, stating, "Moreover, I will give all the wealth of the city, all its gains, all its prized belongings, and all the treasures of the kings of Judah into the hand of their enemies, who shall plunder them and seize them and carry them to Babylon."

> » **What did the Babylonians claim as their own as they besieged the city, according to 2 Kings 24:12–13?**

Along with the temple treasures, the people of Jerusalem were sent to Babylon as captives, with only the poorest of people left to care for the land. Jehoiachin would also be led away with ten thousand others to live in this foreign place.

Zedekiah

While pretending to be loyal to Babylon, Zedekiah took the throne and found a friend in Egypt to wage war against the sure attack of the Babylonians. As Babylon marched to battle, they were confronted by the Egyptians and left Jerusalem to attack them instead.

> » **Jeremiah attempted to warn Zedekiah. What message did he give him in Jeremiah 38:2–3?**

Zedekiah chose not to heed this warning, and he even attempted to gather the surrounding nations to war against Babylon. These efforts were in vain as Nebuchadnezzar would send his men to attack and destroy the city of Jerusalem.

The fate of Zedekiah was already sealed as both Jeremiah and Ezekiel had prophesied. What was the downfall that awaited this king from Jeremiah 34:3 and Ezekiel 12:13?

» How was this prophecy fulfilled, according to 2 Kings 25:6–7?

With the king in chains and the people taken captive, the army of Babylon burned the Lord's temple to the ground and broke down the walls surrounding the city. The words of the prophets had come to pass, and the city was a pile of rubble.

As leaders rise and fall, so do their followers. Such was true of the nation of Israel. Their choice to bow before their own desires and worship gods of a foreign land led them to disaster.

The focus of worship dictates our fate. The people of God found themselves captive because of their blatant disregard for God.

This is the same reality of those who find themselves in a wrong mode of worship even today. When we place another on the throne of our lives, we become captives even within our own homes. As we realize this is happening, the strength that once brought joy from God is shifted to our own strength. We then become devoid of joy, with the gloom of despair filling our heart.

Unleash the Power of Praise:

Recognize the truth found in God's Word that encourages us to worship.

Despair does not have to be a place we reside. We are promised that God not only longs to build the walls of the temple, but also longs to rebuild our lives to the place where we experience His perfect peace.

Read the verses below.

> We have a strong city; he sets up salvation as walls and bulwarks. Open the gates, that the righteous nation that keeps faith may enter in. You keep him in perfect peace whose mind is stayed on you, because he trusts in you. Trust in the Lord forever, for the Lord God is an everlasting rock. (Isaiah 26:1–4)

What hope do you find for the exiles within these words?

What promises do you find for yourself?

What is the key to perfect peace given within Isaiah's words?

How can this key aid you as you rebuild your life of worship?

A woman who walks with Jesus is able to live through both sorrow and joy as she has learned to live fully in her story even with all its brokenness.
—Debbie Alsdorf

WEEK ONE • DAY FOUR

I have lived in the same place almost all my life. My family moved to Arizona when I was just three months old, and although I have lived in several homes, they have all been within a ten-mile radius. Even though I remain planted, many of my friends have not. My best friend from childhood moved to Florida when I was twenty-four. I remember the long flight back after leaving her in her new surroundings like it was yesterday. I sobbed the entire flight. I'm quite certain the people next to me thought I was a complete basket case. They would not have been too far off.

The season after I arrived back home was foreign to me, as I now had to learn to live in a place without my friend with whom I had spent every day of my life. Home didn't look like it used to, and navigating this once familiar place was filled with the unknown. I felt exiled in the place I had lived all my life, my heart longing for something more. The routine of stopping by her workplace, going to dinner and a movie, or just hanging out at home was met with loneliness.

I'm not sure how long it took, but eventually my life became normal again as other friends found their place on my calendar and even within my heart. Although I still missed my dear friend, her exile had found a new normal for me. My friend, on the other hand, had been completely uprooted, just like the exiles were in 586 BC.

Home for God's people was now in a foreign land with an unknown language and a strange culture. They were captive in a country of their enemies, and yet as time went by, they found themselves assimilating into their new surroundings. This captivity was unlike what they expected. The thoughts of being carried away to a foreign land and treated like prisoners brought fear. But as they arrived and time went by, they found themselves simply "living." Captivity had an eerie sense of freedom within their unseen chains—a freedom that allowed them to live, yet also held them hostage from the place they longed to be: home.

> » Jeremiah was taken captive as well. Read Jeremiah 40:2–6 and record what option Jeremiah was given from the Babylonian captain and what he chose to do.

This prophet, Jeremiah, chose to stay back in Jerusalem with the poorest in the land who were left to care for what little still existed in the midst of the rubble. Jeremiah saw with his own eyes the destruction that lay before him, and he knew the prophecy had indeed come true.

A new governor over Judah was appointed, Gedaliah, who instructed the remaining Jews left in the city to follow the commands given by the Babylonian rulers. His reign was cut short, however, because he failed to recognize the danger in not dealing with the enemy, and he was assassinated by a man named Ishmael who wanted the throne. But soon after, Ishmael's attempt to gain the throne was threatened, and he fled for his life.

This is when Johanan took the throne. He was given a word from the Lord by the prophet Jeremiah. Unfortunately, he did not heed the word, and he led the people away from their home to Egypt, taking Jeremiah with him.

God's people were now scattered. More than thirteen hundred miles separated the exiles in Babylon from those who escaped into Egypt. Even so, Jeremiah brought a message from the Lord to those in captivity that provided instruction and reminded them of an awaited promise.

This next passage we will study is one of my favorites in all of Scripture. The promise we claim today may sound familiar, but the surrounding words will bring both instruction and encouragement within our own culture that holds us captive today.

We long to be home in the presence of our heavenly Father! But until that day, here we are on earth, living life the best we know how. Still, within our hearts, we are restless for heaven. Ecclesiastes 3:11 (NIV) reminds us why, for it says, "He has also set eternity in the human heart." We were made for something more, something that lasts forever, and so our hearts are bent toward eternity.

While we wait, we are living as exiles, foreigners on the globe and captive to the world and all the wickedness that surround us. This is not our home—it is our training ground for eternity. How we live and what we learn does make a difference. The words Jeremiah gave to the exiles are words that will show us how to live today. Listen carefully and give them great regard as we study.

Jeremiah 29 is the first recorded letter written in Scripture. The year was 597 BC[1], and the exiles had been in captivity for ten years, some of them longer. Jeremiah was concerned that God's people did not remember the words he gave them regarding their captivity, and he realized that false prophets were spreading rumors that God would bring them into restoration earlier than they had been told. This letter reminded them of their fate and gave them instructions as to their role while they bid their time waiting to be restored.

Read Jeremiah 29:1–14 and answer the following questions.

» **To whom is this letter written, and who delivered the letter to Babylon (vv. 1, 3)?**

» What instructions did Jeremiah give the exiles while they were there (vv. 5–7)?

» What was the promise given if they followed the instructions to seek peace and prosperity for Babylon(v. 7)?

» What admonitions did Jeremiah give the exiles to heed while they were there (vv. 8–9)?

» How long would they live as exiles in Babylon (v. 10)?

» What is the promise of hope given to them after the time is complete (vv. 11–12)?

» What was the condition of this promise coming to pass (vv. 13–14)?

Did you see the verse many people claim because of its beautiful promise? I mean, why wouldn't you want to claim it? Everyone longs for a future filled with hope and void of evil. I know I sure do!

> For I know the plans I have for you, declares the Lord, plans for welfare and not for evil, to give you a future and a hope. (Jeremiah 29:11)

Something happens when we place this verse in context, which means that we study it with all the other verses that surround it. You see, this is a conditional promise. It's the *then* to the *if*. It's a promise that would take seventy years to come to fruition. Most of the people who received this letter would not live to see it to completion.

Unleash the Power of Praise:
Reclaim the blessings of God found as we worship Him alone.

We read in Jeremiah 29:12–14 that the promise is given through the repentance of God's people. We will find next week that the exiles did indeed repent because they are granted access back home. But that repentance came through the process that led to a promise fulfilled.

In the following verses, underline the actions the exiles would take, and circle the responses from God.

> Then you will call upon me and come and pray to me, and I will hear you. You will seek me and find me, when you seek me with all your heart. I will be found by you, declares the Lord, and I will restore your fortunes and gather you from all the nations and all the places where I have driven you, declares the Lord, and I will bring you back to the place from which I sent you into exile. (Jeremiah 29:12–14)

What are the actions you need to take from the above verses?

What blessings does the Lord promise you?

Even in captivity, the exiles were encouraged to worship. Jeremiah's letter begins with how to live in the foreign land physically with the purpose of becoming worshipers of God, even without a temple. The promise to be brought out of captivity and back to their home was the very fuel that ignited their daily existence, knowing one day they would be home.

They knew deliverance was possible and they had hope because of the stories passed down from their ancestors, from as far back as the exodus when God led them out of slavery in Egypt. Perhaps the reminder of the tyranny in Egypt over God's people, as they served as slaves in Pharaoh's court, brought to mind the goodness of God, even when life seemed hopeless. He would deliver them.

The words from the law in the book of Deuteronomy may have brought a familiar message as they read the letter of Jeremiah over and over.

Deuteronomy 6:23 says, "He brought us out from there, that he might bring us in and give us the land that he swore to give to our fathers."

The land now lies in rubble. They may have thought, *If God could do it for them, surely He can do it for us.* Their prayer would then become a cry of, *Do it again, Lord. Do it again!*

Often we are spurred on to keep going by past reminders of God's amazing promises in our life.

Recall a time when God brought you out of a circumstance and led you into something new.

God brought me out of _____

And brought me into _____

Because He has promised to _____

Some of the most difficult and painful seasons of my life have led me to the most beautiful of places. I can still feel the sting of a long and challenging time of ministry.

It seemed it would never end, and to be honest, I just wanted to give up. Through the companionship of some faithful sojourners on the same path, we continued to press on. God sure did deal with a whole lot of *yuck* in my life and in our church, and we needed His chastising that brought us to a place of repentance. He then began to change us and our circumstance. He gave us exactly what He also promised to the exiles—a future filled with hope.

And just when we think all is well and we are comfortable in our surroundings, He begins to move again. Our final *in* will bring us to be *in* His glorious presence. Home.

But while we wait for eternity with Him, we still have living to do, and it's not going to be easy. Jesus told His disciples of life's difficulties: "In this world you will have trouble" (John 16:33 NIV). And even though He is the overcomer of trouble, this trouble is still our reality while we await victory. Just as Jeremiah gave instructions on how to live in captivity, God gives us His Word to guide us on our earthly journey. Our part is obedience!

There will be no peace in any soul until it is willing to obey the voice of God.
—D. L. MOODY

For more information on *events of the exile*, go to caroltetzlaff.com and click on "Ezra Study."

WEEK ONE • DAY FIVE

Reflection and Application

Day Five will be a reflection to seek truth within Scripture as you allow the Holy Spirit to guide you. I recognize this is one day of the study many will choose to skip; in fact, I used to be that girl. I didn't want to think about anything, let alone write down anything, that would remind me of my shortcomings or cause me to have to search past failures, painful memories, shattered dreams, or even sin. And the thought of recording intimate prayers and thoughts on a page someone may actually see was not going to happen. Does anyone resonate with that?

It also just takes a lot of work. It's so much easier to simply read and answer some questions. But if we are going to become women who are willing to sacrificially place our lives on the altar of surrender with the aim to worship God in every part, we have some work to do. This work isn't just about knowing; it's about doing! It's the commitment to rebuild the broken into something beautiful through our worship.

Please allow me to share something I have learned in my own journey. As I began to give permission for the Holy Spirit to really work through Bible study, I was transformed to become more like the image of Jesus, and I have record of it! Looking back at those first years of study, when I forced myself to write a brief word or cryptic statement about the working of the Spirit within me in regard to my past, my present, and even my dreams, a transformation began to take place.

Now as I prayerfully engage with the writings of those God has allowed to guide me through His Word, my words flow like the gushing of Niagara! What began as a guided thought or meditation from the writer flows into streams of transparent scribbling as my heart becomes more and more vulnerable to His directions and promises.

So now, whether you are at the *cryptic message stage of life* or you are ready to *let it flow*, join me—and let's get to the business of the heart and allow the Holy Spirit to speak as we become women ready to listen and follow His leading. Be messy, use lots of color, draw pictures, or just find your medium black-ink pen and begin.

Unleash the Power of Praise:

Reflect on what God is teaching us personally about our worship.

If you're ready, the first thing we are going to do is read aloud from Ephesians. This is my prayer for us.

> I do not cease to give thanks for you, remembering you in my prayers, that the God of our Lord Jesus Christ, the Father of glory, may give you the Spirit of wisdom and of revelation in the knowledge of him, having the eyes of your hearts enlightened, that you may know what is the hope to which he has called you, what are the riches of his glorious inheritance in the saints. (Ephesians 1:16–18)

Now make it personal and use it to launch your own words. He longs to hear your intentions as you commit to allowing the Spirit to move in your heart and mind. Write out the words to your prayer and say them aloud, confirming them to yourself.

Oh, that we would know Him, long to know Him, and seek to know Him! For indeed, He knows us intimately and perfectly. Psalm 139 describes His knowledge so beautifully. Read the words and take them personally. Circle, underline, draw arrows, and highlight those concepts that speak to your soul.

> O Lord, you have searched me and known me!
> You know when I sit down and when I rise up;

you discern my thoughts from afar.

You search out my path and my lying down

and are acquainted with all my ways.

Even before a word is on my tongue,

behold, O Lord, you know it altogether.

You hem me in, behind and before,

and lay your hand upon me.

Such knowledge is too wonderful for me;

it is high; I cannot attain it.

Where shall I go from your Spirit?

Or where shall I flee from your presence?

If I ascend to heaven, you are there!

If I make my bed in Sheol, you are there!

If I take the wings of the morning

and dwell in the uttermost parts of the sea,

even there your hand shall lead me,

and your right hand shall hold me. . . .

How precious to me are your thoughts, O God!

How vast is the sum of them!

If I would count them, they are more than the sand.

I awake, and I am still with you. (Psalm 139:1–10, 17–18)

This psalm opens with the certainty that God has searched us, but the beauty lies in the end as the psalmist cries out for the searching to continue. The acknowledgment of God knowing everything about us should lead us to the same. There is nothing hidden within our heart, which brings us to an honest look at our own self. Everything we have is laid bare before Him.

Search me, O God, and know my heart! Try me and know my thoughts!

And see if there be any grievous way in me, and lead me in the way

everlasting! (Psalm 139:23–24)

Is this your cry? If so, say this prayer back to Him as you grant Him permission to search and reveal to you what lies deep within your heart. Give heed to what

He discloses, and bring those issues back to Him, knowing that the Holy Spirit is going to assist you along the way. Record any thoughts below.

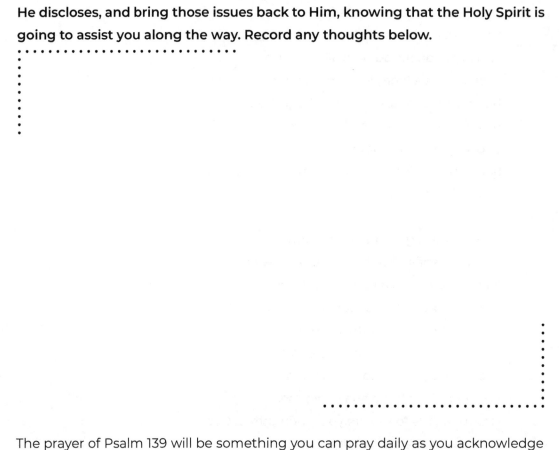

The prayer of Psalm 139 will be something you can pray daily as you acknowledge God's overwhelming desire to transform you.

Think back to the introduction when we looked briefly at Romans 12:1. Read Romans 12:1-2 below and mark the truths that stand out to you.

> I appeal to you therefore, brothers, by the mercies of God, to present your bodies as a living sacrifice, holy and acceptable to God, which is your spiritual worship. Do not be conformed to this world, but be transformed by the renewal of your mind, that by testing you may discern what is the will of God, what is good and acceptable and perfect. (Romans 12:1–2)

In order for us to rebuild a life of worship, as the book of Ezra leads us to do, we must take an inventory of priorities that currently stand in our lives. A worship pastor at my church says, "We all are really good worshipers; the problem is some of us have really bad gods."

Go back to the end of Day Two and recall the mundane task that you noted. Write it again below.

Do you remember your attitudes and emotions as you completed the task? If so, what were they?

You may be thinking, *This is silly; it was just doing laundry. What does doing laundry have to do with worship?*

That's the point! Everything is worship! Even though we equate worship with our heart, it actually begins with our mind. Second Corinthians 10:4 says, "For the weapons of our warfare are not of the flesh but have divine power to destroy strongholds. We destroy arguments and every lofty opinion raised against the knowledge of God, and take every thought captive to obey Christ, being ready to punish every disobedience, when your obedience is complete."

What we think about matters. Whether we are doing laundry, driving carpool, paying bills, or serving the homeless, the thoughts we have during these times fuel our heart of worship. We must train our minds to be taken captive to think toward the things of God. One of the easiest ways to begin this transformation of our minds is simply by being thankful.

What specifically can you be thankful for with the task you completed?

Take a minute to be thankful about the next task that comes before you. It's practicing His presence that leads to proper worship.

I will give thanks to the Lord with my whole heart;
I will recount all of your wonderful deeds.

PSALM 9:1

REVIEW AND DISCUSSION

This portion of the study can be used in two ways. If you are doing this study solo, take the time to answer the questions as a review to what you have experienced in the previous week. If you are doing this study in a group, these questions will lend to group discussion.

Day One

1. How does the inward heart reflect the outward actions as seen in these characters: Cain and Abel, David, the poor widow?
2. What can you learn from the stories that surrounded each of these people?

Day Two

1. Who is the believer's source of victory?
2. What evidence is given to His power?
3. How does His power within us affect our worship?

Day Three

1. What did the kings of Jerusalem have in common after the death of Josiah?
2. Did Jeremiah's words from the Lord help or hinder the nation? How?
3. The only story we have record of during the exile is of Daniel. What do you think his family was thinking as each king came into power before they were taken captive?
4. Is there any correlation to Daniel's experience that you can link to our world today?

Day Four

1. What verse in Jeremiah 29 was a promise of hope for the exiles?
2. What are the conditions of this promise?
3. How does this promise relate to you?

Day Five

1. What are a few things you enjoy doing?
2. What is something you need to do that you would rather never do again?
3. What is the key to finding your heart aligned to God's in the mundane tasks of life?
4. What is your takeaway for this week of study?

TEACHING NOTES

Return

Week Two

WEEK TWO • DAY ONE

Ezra 1:1

Enter Cyrus—the king of Persia, conqueror of nations, and anointed of God!

If that doesn't blow your mind, you may need a little history lesson as to who this man is within the saga of this ancient narrative. Cyrus founded the Persian Empire and conquered one nation at a time until he ruled over southeast Asia. This area included Babylon, where the exiles resided.

Cyrus did not believe in the one true God, but often would name any deity recognized by the people in the realm of his rule to gain ground. He was not a man of faith. He was a politician and did whatever it took to bring his captives to a place where they would follow him. He knew that in order to maintain a strong empire he would need to work with the people rather than against them, and so he had a great idea—one that we see rooted in the providence of God more than two hundred years earlier.

> In the first year of Cyrus king of Persia, that the word of the Lord by the mouth of Jeremiah might be fulfilled, the Lord stirred up the spirit of Cyrus king of Persia, so that he made a proclamation throughout all his kingdom and also put it in writing. (Ezra 1:1)

Not only did Jeremiah prophesy about this moment, but so did Isaiah. Take a look at what Isaiah wrote 210 years before this very moment in history.

Read Isaiah 44:28 along with 45:1–7 and 12–13.

» Write the last two phrases of Isaiah 45:3 below.

   » That you may know _____, the Lord

   » the God of Israel, who call you _____

» Write the last two phrases of Isaiah 45:4 below.

   » I call you by _____

   » I name you, though you _____

» What do you discover about Cryus in these two phrases?

» What truth about our God is communicated in these two phrases?

Even though Cyrus did not know God, God knew him. Not only did He know him, but He used him to fulfill a prophecy—a prophecy that has more references than any other direct prophecy in Scripture. There are 608 prophecies regarding the destruction of Judah, the exile, and the return of the remnant. As Ezra 1:1 came to pass, the prophecy was about to be complete!

Take a look again at Isaiah 45:5–7 and write below the three phrases that begin with the same statement about our God.

I am the LORD _____

I am the LORD _____

I am the LORD _____

God has authority over the entire created order. From the heights of the heavens to the depths of the seas, there is nothing that escapes His knowledge. He is not surprised at the happenings of my life or yours. He knows the score of your life, for He is the master composer. He has divinely orchestrated a magnificent melody that sings the story of your life.

The exiles certainly were not thrilled to be captives and live in the land of their captors. Many of them would die without seeing their home ever again, but it took this drastic measure for them to come to a place of repentance. The graciousness of God reminded them there is a plan that brought hope for their future. The song of their lives had played in a minor key as they endured seventy years of captivity, but the time for God's promise would swell in a grand crescendo as the choice to return was now up to them.

The promise of God's plan is not just an Old Testament truth. Paul writes about this in Romans 8 while chained to a guard and being held under house arrest. This verse is intertwined with the ministry of the Holy Spirit in our lives as it conveys a message we all need to hear in the middle of our disappointments and pain. This message is one of hope.

Take a moment to read Romans 8:26–28.

» **What is the challenge we have in verse 26?**

» **As we begin to see God's will unfold before our eyes, we will come to understand that the promise found in verse 28 is true. Write the promise below.**

God works things for our good and His glory! There have been times when things in my life worked out for good, but I initially didn't view them as good. There are even some things about which I still ask God, *Where is the good in this?* There are outcomes we may never understand until eternity.

This world is filled with all kinds of heartbreak, rejection, disappointment, and pain. It is not always possible to recognize the good found in difficulty, but it is always possible to know that God is good. Not only is it possible, but it is the perfect truth of who He is!

I've experienced great loss in my own life and have recently witnessed friends walk through difficult times of their own. I've watched my best friend lose her husband to cancer after only ten years of marriage. I've walked a wearisome road with friends as their eighteen-month-old little girl lost her battle with a genetic disease. I've come alongside friends as they've struggled with their twenty-year-old daughter living homeless and in addiction. Where is the good in all these circumstances?

I'm quite certain you, too, have a life story to share from your circle of family and friends. To say the outcome is good is like a slap in the face to these precious hearts whose pain is as real today as in the moments of suffering. The one who said "time heals a broken heart" has never experienced great loss. The hopes and dreams of lives lost still exist in the hearts of their loved ones.

There is a ray of light that brings hope during these seasons of dark despair as we rest within the truth that God is good. His goodness is not dependent on the answer to our prayer. God is good! It's a complete sentence, and it's the truth that completes our pain.

Unleash the Power of Praise:

Rediscover the meaning of worship.

Remember the truth that God is good! It's a complete sentence. Let's end our time together by taking some time to simply thank God for His goodness. As you do, do not attempt to tie His goodness to your circumstances. Just simply thank Him. Worship Him today because He is God and, indeed, He is good!

Read Psalm 136. What is the overarching theme that is echoed throughout this song?

> [1] Give thanks to the Lord, for he is good,
>   for his steadfast love endures forever.
> [2] Give thanks to the God of gods,
>   for his steadfast love endures forever.
> [3] Give thanks to the Lord of lords,
>   for his steadfast love endures forever;
> [4] to him who alone does great wonders,
>   for his steadfast love endures forever;
> [5] to him who by understanding made the heavens,
>   for his steadfast love endures forever;
> [6] to him who spread out the earth above the waters,
>   for his steadfast love endures forever;
> [7] to him who made the great lights,
>   for his steadfast love endures forever;
> [8] the sun to rule over the day,
>   for his steadfast love endures forever;
> [9] the moon and stars to rule over the night,

for his steadfast love endures forever;

¹⁰ to him who struck down the firstborn of Egypt,

for his steadfast love endures forever;

¹¹ and brought Israel out from among them,

for his steadfast love endures forever;

¹² with a strong hand and an outstretched arm,

for his steadfast love endures forever;

¹³ to him who divided the Red Sea in two,

for his steadfast love endures forever;

¹⁴ and made Israel pass through the midst of it,

for his steadfast love endures forever;

¹⁵ but overthrew Pharaoh and his host in the Red Sea,

for his steadfast love endures forever;

¹⁶ to him who led his people through the wilderness,

for his steadfast love endures forever;

¹⁷ to him who struck down great kings,

for his steadfast love endures forever;

¹⁸ and killed mighty kings,

for his steadfast love endures forever;

¹⁹ Sihon, king of the Amorites,

for his steadfast love endures forever;

²⁰ and Og, king of Bashan,

for his steadfast love endures forever;

²¹ and gave their land as a heritage,

for his steadfast love endures forever;

²² a heritage to Israel his servant,

for his steadfast love endures forever.

²³ It is he who remembered us in our low estate,

for his steadfast love endures forever;

²⁴ and rescued us from our foes,

for his steadfast love endures forever;

²⁵ he who gives food to all flesh,

for his steadfast love endures forever.

²⁶ Give thanks to the God of heaven,

for his steadfast love endures forever. (Psalm 136:1–26)

What is the overarching theme that is echoed throughout this song?

What attributes of God are found in verse 1?

Take a moment and pray this back to the Father, acknowledging the truth that He is both good and His love endures forever. Use specific circumstances within your own life.

Example: *Father God, Your goodness is made evident to me each morning as I sit across the living room from my husband and see the precious gift You have given me in his encouragement and support of me. The simple cup of coffee we share each day reminds me of Your great love for me.*

When we look deeper into the first verse of this psalm, we see that there is an element of worship that is called out by the psalmist as an action crucial to our success. It is the response we have to the goodness and steadfast love of our Father.

From Psalm 136:1, what is our response?

Take a moment to write out your own song of thankfulness to God. Recall the evidence of His goodness and His love in your life.

God's goodness is the root of all goodness; and our goodness,
if we have any, springs out of His goodness.
—William Tyndale

WEEK TWO • DAY TWO

Ezra 1:2–4

I recently saw a horrible tragedy on the news. A freight train caught fire on a bridge suspended above a man-made lake near Arizona State University. The front car derailed and was hanging over the side of bridge, with the rest of the train covered in flames. Black smoke billowed as far as the eye could see. It wasn't too long until parts of the bridge began to collapse, putting everyone in the area in danger.

One couple told the reporters they were just about to walk underneath when they heard a loud crack and saw pieces of the bridge falling in their path. Destruction was all around them, and they had to back away quickly to escape.

Devastating sights and sounds have become an ordinary part of our days. Anything happening in our world can be seen in real time as the media feeds it to us by every possible means of communication. We no longer need to use our imaginations, for the images we see tell the stories, and we realize devastation is, indeed, all around us.

The scene we will look at today depicts the people of God taken captive. Although the images are not clear to us, many of the exiles in our storyline would still remember the horrific night when the armies of Babylon laid siege to their city and forced them to leave everything behind to journey to a foreign land.

Oftentimes we read the narrative of Scripture as simple fact without thinking about the feeling and emotions involved, but today I want you to sense the fear that overwhelmed the people as their homes were ransacked one by one, their families were torn apart, and their temple was burned. Imagine the scene as if it was broadcast across the airways on our media outlets.

Read Joel 2:6–9 that describes the day of the Lord's judgment on Judah.

» **From this prophetic description, what images would be broadcast on the screen as this event was realized?**

» We get a glimpse into the soul of these Babylonian exiles when we read Psalm 137:1–9. Read the psalm and describe the scene and the emotional state of these captives.

The devastation of their homes did not even compare to the devastation of their souls. These were a people who were broken, afraid, and ready to give up the fight. The cry of their song was one of desperation. They couldn't return and change the past, yet moving forward seemed hopelessly impossible.

Think back to a circumstance or season of your life that brought a sense of hopelessness. Those same feelings were in the soul of the exiles as they were forced to live in a foreign land.

After seventy years of captivity, the sting of bondage may have worn off a bit as the people assimilated into the foreign culture. They were foreigners still, yet they found a place to call home. Many would have been born during this time of captivity and only heard the stories of their capture, yet others longed to go home and could vividly remember Solomon's temple in all its glory. They were told the opportunity to return home would happen when the seventy years were complete, but did they really believe it?

The prophet Isaiah tells of this very day in the midst of his message that speaks first to their destruction. Seventy years separated the prophecies given in Isaiah 9:13 and Isaiah 10:20–21. Take a moment to read both the ESV and the NLT to gain understanding.

» Read the passages and compare the attitudes and actions of the people of Israel from the time of their capture to the time of their release.

It took seventy years for their hearts to be moved back toward God—seventy years of hardship in a foreign land away from the Lord, the Holy One of Israel.

I have seen many rebellious hearts wallow in defiance before turning back to God, including my own. And I've watched from a distance and have seen people who just can't seem to find their sin distasteful enough to repent for a very, very, very long time! Can you relate? Maybe it's your child, a family member, a friend, a teenager, or maybe it's even you. If we're completely honest, we must admit this rebellion has been found in our own hearts.

Thanks be to God for always pursuing us to the point of pain to bring us back to Him.

When we are far away from home, He longs for us to return, and that is just what is about to happen to our exiles as they look to a day when their release will come.

That's where the story of Ezra picks up as King Cyrus is about to make a proclamation that will change their lives once again!

Read Ezra 1:2–4

» **What title does Cyrus give to God?**

» **What does Cyrus say he has been given from God?**

» **What does Cyrus say God asked him to do?**

» **What does Cyrus remind the people about their God?**

» **What two things does Cyrus tell the people to do?**

» **The title Cyrus gives God in verse 2 is met with another location as to where God resides. Where does he say God dwells in verse 3?**

» Looking at these statements from this pagan king, what do you surmise are his thoughts about the God of Israel?

» How would this act of allowing the exiles to return to Jerusalem and rebuild their temple benefit Cyrus?

You who were once held captive are released! You are free to go and worship your God. These words must have been music to their ears. For a people whose worship centered around their temple, there would be nothing more glorious than to return home and rebuild.

Unleash the Power of Praise:

Realize the challenges found in our misalignment of our worship of God.

As the decree from Cyrus became widespread in the Jewish community, discussions in their homes must have been filled with wonder as the opportunity to return was in reach. Even so, we will find that many chose to stay in the city that held them captive. The comfort of their captivity had become home, and complacency had taken rule in their hearts. They may have still fostered a love for God, but the inconvenience of uprooting their family and way of life may had taken precedence. When the worship of the Holy One is misaligned, it brings challenges within choices.

Yet we will read of the others who chose to return. The conversations in their homes when the declaration was realized brought hope. The promise Jeremiah had given them had come true. This was the day they had been waiting for, and they were ready to return.

I wonder if this song of King David echoed in the hearts of those who began to pack their things as the words from Psalm 122 flooded their homes.

Read Psalm 122 and imagine yourself telling your family about the news you just heard.

> I was glad when they said to me,
> "Let us go to the house of the Lord!"
> Our feet have been standing
> within your gates, O Jerusalem!
> Jerusalem—built as a city
> that is bound firmly together,
> to which the tribes go up,
> the tribes of the Lord,
> as was decreed for Israel,
> to give thanks to the name of the Lord.
> There thrones for judgment were set,
> the thrones of the house of David.
> Pray for the peace of Jerusalem!
> "May they be secure who love you!
> Peace be within your walls
> and security within your towers!"
> For my brothers and companions' sake
> I will say, "Peace be within you!"
> For the sake of the house of the Lord our God,
> I will seek your good. (Psalm 122:1–9)

From this psalm, what was their response to their future of freedom?

What was their prayer?

Soon they would begin the journey home, and their restless hearts would know peace and gladness once again.

What are you longing for that makes your heart restless?

Seek the heart of the Father to determine if your restlessness is caused by a misalignment of your worship. Write your thoughts below. Remember that He alone will bring peace to your heart, just as He did to the exiles as they were obedient to return to the house of the Lord.

You have made us for Yourself, and our heart is restless until it rests in You.
—Augustine

For more information on *Cyrus Cylinder*, go to caroltetzlaff.com and click on "Ezra Study."

WEEK TWO • DAY THREE

Ezra 1:5–11

The people of God did not return to Jerusalem empty-handed. The artifacts used in the temple were returned to them before their journey began. But how did the Babylonians become the possessor of these items? It's found in the story of Hezekiah.

A grave mistake was made during Hezekiah's reign in Judah. We are told in 2 Kings 20 that the king of Babylon sent a message and gifts to King Hezekiah because he had been ill. This appearance of kindness moved Hezekiah to show them all the temple riches and treasures.

Second Chronicles 32:31 reveals to us this was a testing of his heart: "And so in the matter of the envoys of the princes of Babylon, who had been sent to him to inquire about the sign that had been done in the land, God left him to himself, in order to test him and to know all that was in his heart."

We discover that Hezekiah was one of the few kings of Judah who followed after God's way for the kingdom. What does 2 Kings 18:5–7 tell you about King Hezekiah?

If Hezekiah was committed to God, why would he take it upon himself to show the enemy the kingdom of Judah and all its treasure? Pride!

He had seen success during his reign and had even experienced a miraculous healing. He defeated the Assyrians, so why not go further and show the Babylonian enemies how wealthy his kingdom was? Surely this would show his great power. His actions disclosed the depth of his prideful heart and revealed the perception that he was indispensable and that nothing could touch him.

He failed the test, and this arrogant display was the catalyst that enticed the king of Babylon to conquer Judah without fail. This is fulfilled in 2 Kings 25 as King Nebuchadnezzar, the king of Babylon, arrived in Jerusalem with a vengeance. He burned down the temple, destroyed the walls around the city, took the temple treasures, and left the city in ruins.

At this time the priests and people of the land felt completely violated, but God had a plan to preserve it all! Through the seventy years of captivity, the treasures of the temple were safely stored away, only to make a brief appearance during the reign of King Belshazzar.

During his reign over Babylon, Belshazzar held a feast and commanded that the vessels his father had taken from the temple in Jerusalem be brought out so that they could use them. Let's just say that was a big mistake (Daniel 5).

With the temple artifacts back in storage, we are ready to join our exiles right where we left them, packing their belonging to return home.

Read Ezra 1:5–11.

If you do quick math, you will find that the numbers just don't add up. Only 2,499 pieces are accounted for in this list. But don't dismay! The only ones mentioned by number in the text are the larger vessels. Many smaller items were returned as well, though unlisted.

» **What similarities do the movement of the people and the proclamation of King Cyrus have in common? Compare with Ezra 1:1.**

» **God was stirring, and His people were ready to move. Even those who did not sense the Spirit leading them to return to Jerusalem did their part. How did they assist those who were preparing to leave?**

» **How does King Cyrus assist the returning exiles?**

King Cyrus had just fulfilled another prophecy given by Jeremiah as he returned the temple artifacts to God's people. The prophecy is found in Jeremiah 27:21–22.

» **What was the crucial element necessary to the return of these vessels?**

You may remember from Week One that Jeremiah warned the people that some would give false hope regarding both the length of their captivity and the return of their belongings. Hananiah was one such prophet. You can read about him in Jeremiah 28.

Hananiah came before the people and contradicted Jeremiah's words. He brought the message that in just two years, the king of Babylon—Nebuchadnezzar at this time—would be destroyed and all the temple vessels would be returned. He also spoke to the return of all the exiles who were taken to Babylon. The scary thing was that the people believed him. They put their trust in a lie, and God took Hananiah's life just two months later.

Jeremiah warned the people again that the seventy years would be complete before they would be allowed to return with their belongings. Hananiah must not have been the only one deceiving the people during their captivity.

» **Write down the warning in Jeremiah 29:8–10 regarding this circumstance.**

Unleash the Power of Praise:
Recognize the truths found in God's Word that encourage us to worship.

What promises do we see unfolding in our exiles' story in Ezra 1?

It's God's plan in God's time! As the exiles prepared their belongings to begin the journey to Jerusalem, they experienced God's promise firsthand. The excitement of returning home with the temple treasures secured for the journey may have been just the assurance they needed for what lay ahead.

The fulfillment of God's promise encouraged them to recognize the truth that God was indeed with them. His Spirit had moved them, and they were on their way home!

The truth we discovered from Romans 8:28 on Day One is evident in the lives of our exiles. Indeed, God does work everything together for good. The confiscation of the temple artifacts may have resulted in the disobedience of King Hezekiah, but God used it for His greater plan.

With the temple artifacts securely hidden in Babylon, the people had everything they needed to restore their worship once the temple was rebuilt. God's promise was kept; His truth was fulfilled.

What promise do you need to claim today?

Do you believe God is faithful to keep His promise?

Reflect on the words in Joshua 21:45 (NIV): "Not one of all the Lord's good promises to Israel failed; every one was fulfilled."

Write out your response to this truth as you cling to the promises of God in your life.

From one end of the Bible until the other, God assures us that
He'll never go back on His promises.
—BILLY GRAHAM

WEEK TWO • DAY FOUR

Ezra 2:1–70

Marie Rose Abad	Robert Levine	Maria Ramirez
Shannon Lewis Adams	Terence M. Lynch	Paul F. Sarle
Robert J. Baierwalter	Joseph P. McDonald	Kenneth Tietjen
John A. Cooper	Karen Susan Navarro	Mary Alice Wahlstrom
Pamela Lee Gaff	Robert Parro	Kevin Patrick York

*toledoblade.com, September 10, 2011, The Blade, Associated Press

Did you read through the names listed above, or did you just briefly look to see if anyone was listed who you might know and then quickly move on? The list above may receive a bit more of your interest when the names are placed in context. This is just a small sampling of names of the 2,977 people who were murdered in the terrorist attack of September 11, 2001. When we take a moment to find out who they are, the list takes on a whole new meaning. Robert Parro was part of the New York City Fire Department and was sent to the World Trade Center on a rescue mission. He was thirty-five years old. Terrence M. Lynch was forty-nine years old and was with the United States Army. He was doing a contract job at the Pentagon. Shannon Adams was only twenty-five years old and was working in the World Trade Center.

Typically, when we see a list of names, we look for the one that brings some recognition and dismiss the rest. I mean, who has time to read through a list of names containing people you don't even know?

The names of these people are all connected to family and friends who continue to mourn their death and still grieve over the loss of their dreams for them.

As you glance over chapter 2 of the book of Ezra, you will find another list of names and numbers. This chapter may be one that you would typically scan over briefly without real thought of who these people actually were, but each of these people have a place in the epic history of God's people as an amazing prophecy is fulfilled.

I want to encourage you to read through chapter 2 of Ezra. There are many difficult names to pronounce, and I have found it easier to digest with apps or websites that read the passage aloud.

These are two resources that will read the chapter to you:
» App: Bible (YouVersion)
» Website: biblegateway.com

Read or listen to Ezra 2.

» According to verse 1, who took them captive, and where did they live during the captivity?

» To which place are the captives returning?

» The city of _____ in the land of _____, each to his own _____.

» What clues does that statement give about where the people will settle?

» Who is leading the return of the exiles? (Hint: his name is listed first.)

» Why do you think it is important for the leaders who are bringing the exiles to Jerusalem to rebuild the temple to have an accurate list of who is going with them? In other words, why does the ancestry of the people even matter?

The list of people is divided with much purpose. Fill in the blanks to recognize who is returning with Zerubbabel.

» The number of the _____ of the people of _____ (vv. 3–35).

   » What is significant about this location?

   » Why do you think the location listed shifted from Judah?

   » What change takes place in the list between verses 19–20?

The next section indicates the servants of the temple divided by function.

» The _____ (vv. 36–39)

» The _____ (v. 40)

» The _____ (v. 41)

» The _____ (v. 42)

» The _____ _____ (vv. 43–54)

» Solomon's _____ (vv. 55–58)

» In verses 59–63 we find another list of people who are returning with the exiles. What is the issue they are facing?

» What would need to take place in order for them to perform the duties of the priesthood?

» What is the first thing the people do when they arrive in Jerusalem, according to verses 68–69?

» Compare what is given with who is giving in Nehemiah 7:70–72.

	Ezra 2:68–69	Nehemiah 7:70–72
darics of gold	_____	_____
minas of silver	_____	_____
priests' garment	_____	_____

» What does this tell you about both the leaders and the people who returned to Jerusalem?

Unleash the Power of Praise:

Reclaim the blessing of God found as we worship Him alone.

As the people arrived in Jerusalem, the first thing they did was to give an offering. They had just traveled more than nine hundred miles on foot to arrive in a land that had been completely destroyed. Instead of becoming discouraged and walking away from the rubble, they recognized the potential around them and gave to a greater cause—God's work!

God's work not only had been experienced as they traveled safely back home, but was also yet to be experienced. They saw the task before them, as the temple reconstruction would take much effort, but God had a greater work in mind—the work within their hearts.

The giving, both small and great, was an indicator of their tired and weary hearts. Jesus tells us, "For where your treasure is, there your heart will be also" (Matthew 6:21). Their hearts were aligned to the Father as they moved forward to accomplish the great task before them.

What are the instructions about giving found in 2 Corinthians 9:6–8?

What is the result of giving?

How is giving an act of worship?

Psalm 116 is a psalm of great thankfulness and surrender. Although the exact time frame of this psalm is unknown, the words echo a generous heart. Imagine this song being sung by the people as they arrived in Jerusalem. Their worn and tired faces rose to the heavens as they lifted their voices in worship. The response could only result in one action—an offering to the Lord.

> What can I offer the Lord
> for all he has done for me?
> I will lift up the cup of salvation
> and praise the Lord's name for saving me.
> I will keep my promises to the Lord

in the presence of all his people.

The Lord cares deeply

when his loved ones die.

O Lord, I am your servant;

yes, I am your servant, born into your household;

you have freed me from my chains.

I will offer you a sacrifice of thanksgiving

and call on the name of the Lord.

I will fulfill my vows to the Lord

in the presence of all his people—

in the house of the Lord

in the heart of Jerusalem.

Praise the Lord! (Psalm 116:12–19 NLT)

Reread the psalm again, but this time as a prayer from your soul. As you do, write your offering of praise to the Lord next to each portion. As the Holy Spirit begins to move, you may be inclined to give so much more. This is the practice of rebuilding your life of worship!

> *When God blesses you financially, don't raise your standard of living.*
> *Raise your standard of giving.*
> —MARK BATTERSON

WEEK TWO • DAY FIVE

Reflection and Application

The narrative of the exiles' miraculous release and return to Jerusalem has been our focus this week. We were given details of their release—from the number of temple artifacts to the names of people who chose to return, and even the amount given in their offerings—but did you notice that something was missing? It's an event that could have been placed between Ezra 2:64–67 and Ezra 2:68.

Read these verses. Is there anything else you would like to know?

The account ends with a bunch of camels and donkeys that land immediately in Jerusalem, without any mention of how they got there. The nine-hundred-mile trip would have taken at least four months, yet there is no information chronicling their journey! We read of their starting point in Babylon and we know they arrived in Jerusalem, but the adventure between the two is missing.

I guess the writer of the text simply did not find their travel experience worth mentioning because there is a more important matter that must take place. In the divinely inspired Word, we are given exactly what we need to know, for the passage tells us where they have been, who is with them, when they arrived, and what they did.

They worshiped!

There are many elements to planning corporate worship that most people never think about as they engage in worship during a service. As a worship leader, it's my job to consider many factors. How much time do we have? What songs should we sing? What key is singable and will flow seamlessly? What about videos, backgrounds, lights, sound, Scripture? So much goes into the planning each week. The most important thing is that people walking into our services find a connection with God through the elements used in the service.

You see, our journey should always lead us to worship!

Unleash the Power of Praise:

Reflect on what God is teaching you personally about our worship.

What journey are you currently facing right now in your own life?

Are you a mom who is just trying to figure out how to get through the day with the demands of children who need attention, a house that needs a good cleaning, and an empty refrigerator?

Maybe you're working in a job that is just a means of survival.

Are you are facing an illness?

You may be living your best life, retired and spending your days with friends at the community pool.

Maybe you're planning a wedding or preparing for the birth of a child or the funeral of a loved one.

We are all on unique paths, but our journeys have one thing in common—they lead us to worship!

Whether we are praising God in the sunshine or in the storms, our lives are meant to worship Him alone. When our focus is on God and His greatness, His promises, and His love for us, the stuff in our lives is given proper perspective.

Do you remember what the people did as soon as they arrived in Jerusalem? They gave an offering! They worshiped God with all they had. They didn't get to Jerusalem and say, "You know, God, the expenses for this trip really took a toll on my bank account," or, "Do you know the price of hay to fuel these donkeys? I need first and last month's rent to get into my new condo, and Johnny needs new shoes. His soles are all worn out from walking nine hundred miles."

I'm not saying there wasn't any grumbling or complaining. The whole book of Exodus is about God's people whining about their journey. But this is not where God wants us to place our focus. He wants us to know two things: He guided the exiles in their journey, and they responded in worship.

Let's take a moment to reflect on our own lives. What changes or circumstances have you gone through in the past few months?
    . . . in your family?
    . . . in your work?
    . . . in your church?

How have you entrusted these circumstances to God?

What has been your expression of worship through the happenings in your life?

Remember, worship isn't about music. Worship is about a life that is surrendered to God. As we continue the story of the exiles rebuilding a life of worship, we will see in the coming weeks how a life of worship is both hindered and heightened.

> *Whether you are eating or drinking, or whatever you are doing:*
> *do it all for God's glory.*
>
> 1 Corinthians 10:31, paraphrased

That is worship!

REVIEW AND DISCUSSION

Day One

1. What important role did King Cyrus play in the history of the exiles? Discuss the goodness of God within His plan.
2. How do you experience the goodness of God in your life? What effect does this have on your worship?

Day Two

1. What was the reality of the circumstances surrounding the siege of Jerusalem, the journey to Babylon, and life as captives?
2. What promise did the exiles cling to during this time?
3. Think back to a circumstance or season of your life that brought a sense of hopelessness. What were the details surrounding this event?
4. What promises did you cling to during this time?

Day Three

1. What grave mistake did King Hezekiah make, and how did it affect the kingdom of Judah?
2. How did God reverse this mistake for the good of the people and for His glory?
3. How were God's promises ignored by the false prophet Hananiah?
4. What happens when we find ourselves ignoring God's promises?

Day Four

1. Why is the list of people who returned to Jerusalem important to the rebuilding of the temple?
2. What was the first response of the people when they arrived in Jerusalem? How does this display a heart of worship?

Day Five

1. What is your daily practice of worship in the everyday routine of life?
2. What is your takeaway for this week of study?

TEACHING NOTES

_____

_____

_____

_____

_____

_____

_____

_____

_____

_____

_____

_____

_____

_____

_____

_____

_____

_____

_____

Rebuild

Week Three

WEEK THREE • DAY ONE

Ezra 3:1–7

In just thirty years, the farm community I live in has grown from thirty thousand people to over two hundred and fifty thousand people. I still remember the two-lane roads and small local businesses that graced the quaint downtown. Today the wide streets are littered with stores and restaurants, including schools in every community. The migration of people to our town has transformed the place we call home into a vibrant city. The gradual movement of people changed the landscape of our world so slowly that we didn't even realize it was happening.

This was not the case in the city of Jerusalem. The massive entourage of sixty thousand people all arrived at once, and I'm certain it set the inhabitants spinning.

Our third week of study begins with Jerusalem and the surrounding cities that have now been occupied by the exiles for three months. The foreigners who had taken up residence in these locations probably felt a bit pushed out as the people of God thrust themselves back into the towns where their ancestors had lived.

Settling into a new life back home required more than just setting up house. The former traditions that were forgotten in Babylon would now reappear as feast season was upon them.

Read Ezra 3:1–7 to discover how they reintroduced their Jewish customs back into their lives.

The seventh month is Tishri, which is our September and October. The first day of Tishri is the Jewish New Year, or Rosh Hashanah.

The custom for celebration was established by Moses in Leviticus 23:24–25, which says: "In the seventh month, on the first day of the month, you shall observe a day of solemn rest, a memorial proclaimed with blast of trumpets, a holy convocation. You shall not do any ordinary work, and you shall present a food offering to the Lord."

» **How did the people gather from the towns (v. 1)?**

» **What does that specific phrase tell you about their mindset?**

» **What was their first priority to build as they gathered (v. 3)?**

» **What reason does the text give for the people building the altar first?**

Let's take a moment to explore this further. Unlike our corporate worship today, the Jewish people were dependent upon their traditions to worship God as He instructed. God had given very specific commands that would prepare their hearts for a time when the Messiah would come and the traditions of their past would be fulfilled.

Hebrews 9:13–14 explains this fulfillment: "For if the blood of goats and bulls, and the sprinkling of defiled persons with the ashes of a heifer, sanctify for the purification of the flesh, how much more will the blood of Christ, who through the eternal Spirit offered himself without blemish to God, purify our conscience from dead works to serve the living God."

The exiles were part of the Old Testament and were following after the traditions that were handed down by their ancestors during the time of the exodus.

As the children of Israel journeyed through the wilderness from Egypt, they built a tabernacle to house the presence of the Lord. Whenever they moved, they would take the tabernacle apart and then rebuild it when they reached the next point on the journey. However, when the children of Israel crossed the Jordan into the promised land, their first priority was not the tabernacle.

Read Deuteronomy 27:4–6.

» **Why do you think building the altar was their priority?**

In both circumstances, the land was filled with foreigners who worshiped pagan gods.

According to Deuteronomy 20, when God's people entered the promised land, they were given two sets of instructions. First they were given instructions for those cities outside of the land of promise: if the people responded peaceably to the children of Israel, they would live. The second set of instructions included the nations that lived within the boundaries of the promised land.

Read Deuteronomy 20:16–18.

> » **What were the instructions given for those who lived within the boundaries of the promised land?**

> » **What was the reason behind their destruction?**

After the initial conquest of the promised land, Joshua died. Read the following verses from Judges 1 to grasp the progress of the tribes as they sought to take the land. (For a more complete understanding, read the entire chapter of Judges 1.)

Read Judges 1:8, 10, 17, 27, 29, 31, 33, and 34.

> » **What do these verses tell you about their obedience to finish the work they had begun throughout Joshua's leadership?**

> » **Why do you think this happened?**

> » **Where did God's people find success, and what tribes continued in obedience?**

» How does the obedience of some of the tribes from the book of Judges affect the story line in Ezra thus far?

» After doing this bit of research, why do you think the building of the altar was such a priority to the exiles?

We read in the rest of the passage that with the altar built, they were then able to continue the sacrifices and feasts according to the law given by Moses. This was crucial to reestablishing their worship among the foreigners who had taken up residence in their land. But the work had only just begun. It appears that the people, amid their celebrations, had neglected the greater task at hand.

» What does Ezra 3:6 state as the object of their neglect?

» When they recognized this, what did they begin to do to see that it was accomplished (v. 7)?

» How were they able to acquire the supplies needed for rebuilding?

God continued to provide for His people even before the work began. As the supplies for the next stage of their building were acquired, the people needed to remain focused on God in order to accomplish the task that awaited them.

Unleash the Power of Praise:

Rediscover the meaning of worship.

In order for worship to occur, we must recognize those things that take our focus off God and off what He asks us to do. He provides all we need for authentic worship because all we really need is Him. God alone is the only object of our desire. When we focus on Him, our life falls into balance. Whether times are good or things are just plain hard, those who have their eyes upon the Lord will prevail.

The exiles kept their eyes on the task at hand, at least for the moment. Their worship was not just sacrifices on the altar. Their worship was in their work.

Hebrews 12:1–2 explains this truth. "Therefore, since we are surrounded by so great a cloud of witnesses, let us also lay aside every weight, and sin which clings so closely, and let us run with endurance the race that is set before us, looking to Jesus, the founder and perfecter of our faith, who for the joy that was set before him endured the cross, despising the shame, and is seated at the right hand of the throne of God."

What are we to lay aside?

What are we to do?

Who is our motivation?

The race we have been given looks different for each one of us, and yet the preparation and outcome is the same. In every season of our life when we run in obedience the way God has directed, it is worship.

What race are you running in this season of life? This is the thing that takes up your time and energy.

What does it look like to run your current race in obedience within a life of worship?

Write a prayer below asking God to make you aware of His calling toward your obedience in the race you are running. Also ask Him to give you an awareness to remain focused on Him.

Therefore, holy brothers, you who share in a heavenly calling, consider Jesus.

Hebrews 3:1

For more information on *Jewish Festivals*, go to caroltetzlaff.com and click on "Ezra Study."

WEEK THREE • DAY TWO

Ezra 3:8–13

The second month is Ziv, which occurs in the spring during our April–May calendar. This is the same time of year that Solomon built the first temple according to 1 Kings 6:1: "In the four hundred and eightieth year after the people of Israel came out of the land of Egypt, in the fourth year of Solomon's reign over Israel, in the month of Ziv, which is the second month, he began to build the house of the Lord."

Supplies were gathered and the clock was ticking. We find ourselves now in year two of the return to Jerusalem, and yet the foundation of the temple has not been laid.

When I first read this, I thought to myself, *What's the problem? God has given them a task, so what's taking so long?* Gathering supplies is not an easy job. The cedar trees that were used to build the temple could grow to more than 120 feet tall and 30–40 feet in circumference. Those are some pretty mammoth pieces of wood to be cut down and floated on rafts from Phoenicia (modern-day Lebanon) to the port just north of Joppa.

For maps and other resources to enhance this study, go to caroltetzlaff.com.

The supplies needed to start this monumental task would take months. Wood had to be transported by raft and then transferred to carts, pulled by oxen or other livestock, to the city of Jerusalem. As we look at the time stamp of our next section, we know that another seven months had passed.

Read Ezra 3:8–9.

» **Discover the concept found in Ezra 3:1, which is seen twice in this passage.**

» **Why is this so important in completing the work God has given to them?**

» **Read the verses listed below. How did the age limit of a temple servant morph through the years?**

» Numbers 4:2–3

» Numbers 8:24–25

» Ezra 3:8

» What reason can you give for the younger age requirement in the later years?

» What does that tell you about the age demographics of the returned exiles? It may seem like an irrelevant observation, but it will make sense as we continue to read.

Read Ezra 3:10–13.

» The foundation for the temple was laid! What did the people do (v. 10)?

» Who was included in this celebration (v. 11)?

There is a theme of unity found within this chapter:
Verse 1: the people gathered together
Verse 9: the people worked together
Verse 11: the people praise together

» What were the qualities of those who found success when working together, and what was the result as seen in Philippians 2:2?

» When was the last time you saw God's people come together with one mind and the same love to complete a task? What was the result?

The people rejoiced. But if you read a bit closer, you will find that not quite everyone was as excited about the foundation being laid.

» Who responded in a different way, and what was their response? Why?

» What was the focus of the older men?

» What was the focus of the others?

» How did each group of people display a misplaced focus?

» Where should their focus have been directed?

In order for the older men to realize that this foundation was not as glorious as the former temple, they had to have seen Solomon's temple. This indicates they were in Jerusalem before the Babylonian captivity. Do you remember why the Babylonians captured the Jews and took them into exile? It was because of their disobedience. They were warned countless times by the prophets to turn from their wickedness and idolatry and to worship only God. Yet when they did not repent, the inevitable happened! The prophecies came true, and they were taken into captivity. It was the sin of the old men that ultimately destroyed the temple. Throughout the history of Israel, we read the historical accounts of false prophets compromising the temple worship.

Even so, they longed for the glory of that temple to return—the very temple they blasphemed.

I guess they only remembered the grandeur of a building but had forgotten about the God whom they chose to rebel against. They might just have recognized that the good oledays weren't really that good if they took the time to remember the rebellious hearts that turned to pagan gods in worship.

Within the narrative of Ezra, as well as in the church today, problems may occur when two worlds collide: the focus of the *older generation* on the past and the *younger generation* on the present. The selfish outlook in both cases will make for a disaster in the days to come if trouble should ever arise. And I think it just might!

It seems the togetherness that brought about the altar and then the foundation had dissipated in their praise. A facade of unity was heard as loud shouts resonated in the distance, but the fade to silence in the morning light would bring a conflict they were not ready to wield.

» If you were among the crowd and recognized the trouble they were in as their cries divided them, what advice would you give to the old? To the young?

» Do you have a modern-day example where conflicts rise between old and young in the church?

» Read Colossians 3:12–17. What are the instructions that Paul gives to help us know how to navigate these conflicts, and what hope do these instructions bring?

Unleash the Power of Praise:

Realize the challenges found in the misalignment of our worship of God.

Sometimes worship is just noise! That's a scary thought.

Coming together to lift our voices in praise can be void of true worship if our hearts are not focused toward God. Recognizing the object of your praise is crucial to authentic, corporate worship. That kind of worship lays aside our preferences in the past and the present and lifts our words upward to the only One who is worthy to receive them. It is for God alone! There is no one else like Him!

Is there an area in your life where your opinions differ from others in the body of Christ? Identify this area and list it below. Some of the common ones are music styles, preaching styles, interpretation of nonessential doctrines, the administration of Bible study groups, and so much more.

Essential doctrines are things we hold fast to as believers, such as the inerrancy of Scripture, the virgin birth, the Trinity, the return of Christ, salvation by Jesus alone, etc. Nonessential doctrines are things such as how often your church practices communion, the gifts of the Spirit that are active today, and one's view on the rapture, to name a few.

Take a moment and bring these doctrines before Holy God. Ask Him to give you wisdom as you lay down those things that may differ from others based on scriptural interpretation. Write your prayer and thoughts below.

It is the pleasing of God that is at the heart of our worship.
—R. C. SPROUL

WEEK THREE • DAY THREE

Ezra 4:1–5

The shouts of praise ceased for the moment, and the work of building resumed. The walls of the temple were going up, and soon the house of the Lord would be completed. Well, maybe not as soon as hoped!

Read Ezra 4:1–5.

Before we discuss the conflict at hand, let's take a moment to find out who these people are who are called the "adversaries of Judah and Benjamin."

After King Solomon's reign, the kingdom divided into the northern kingdom of Israel, whose capital was Samaria, and the southern kingdom of Judah, whose capital was Jerusalem. The only two tribes who remained loyal to King Rehoboam were Judah and Benjamin. The other ten tribes rebelled and formed the northern kingdom.

The tribes of the northern kingdom were taken into captivity in 722 BC when they fell to Assyria with the conquest of Samaria.

The Assyrian kings imported inhabitants from Mesopotamia and Syria to populate the land they had conquered.

Read 2 Kings 17:24–33.

» **What happened to the people who were sent to live in the cities of Samaria? Why?**

» **What was the solution the king of Assyria decided upon?**

» **What was the result of their worship?**

These were the people who were coming to Jerusalem to inquire about assisting with the rebuilding of the temple. When we read the text, we know right away that they were enemies because we are informed of that in the first sentence, but the people didn't get the benefit of knowing this information. The men of Samaria didn't come to them and say, "Hey, we're the people from Samaria who want to destroy everything you have set out to do. How about you let us join you?"

» **What did the men of Samaria say to Zerubbabel to entice him to accept their help?**

» **What was the response of Zerubbabel and the other leaders to their request, and how did they leverage the command of King Cyrus?**

» **What was the response of the men of Samaria to their dismissal?**

» **How did the builders of the temple react to the tactics of the enemy?**

The Enemy will always scheme to find a way to stop the work that God is doing. Zerubbabel and the leaders were confronted with the choice to accept help in their building project. Don't you think it would have been beneficial to have an extra set of hands to raise the roof of the temple? The work could have been done twice as fast, and the completion of the temple would have been accomplished ahead of schedule.

But the leaders knew God had this task set aside just for them. There were certain specifications to be followed for the house of the Lord to be complete, with each step followed perfectly so the temple could function in the manner in which the sacrifices could take place. The first temple, built by Solomon, took seven years to complete, and so this task was not one to happen quickly. But it would happen, because man cannot thwart the purposes of God.

The choice to not accept the help of the people of Samaria was wise, for the leaders kept their focus on God's task before them. But the people of Samaria did not relent. Their ruthless treatment of the builders terrified them. Think about what had happened within their history. Foreigners had come into their city before and had taken them captive, while all they had burned to the ground. Now the enemy was attacking again, but this time it seemed with their words.

Whoever said the statement, "Sticks and stones will break my bones, but words will never hurt me" never experienced a vicious speech from an enemy. Words can destroy the mind and the soul, sometimes beyond repair. A slap to the face will sting for a moment, but a scourging of the soul will last a lifetime.

> » **Have you ever experienced words that destroyed you more severely than a beating ever would?**

> » **How have you seen the church "destroyed" by words of outsiders?**

Unleash the Power of Praise:

Recognize the truths found in God's Word that encourage us to worship.

We should expect words of destruction from those in the world. Jesus tells us, "In the world you will have tribulation. But take heart; I have overcome the world" (John 16:33). This was a promise to His disciples when He warned them of a time they would be scattered and abandoned. But Jesus told them that even when trouble comes, His peace would be in them.

This same promise is ours to claim and will propel us to continue to live a life of worship.

What precautions can you take so that when the Enemy attacks you, you are not found alone and vulnerable to his assault?

Thank God for the peace that He has promised to give in times of difficulty.

God is faithful and He will overcome. Do not fear!

God, being who He is, cannot cease to be what He is, and being what He is, He cannot act out of character with Himself. He is at once faithful and immutable [unchanging], so all His words and acts must be and must remain faithful.
—A. W. Tozer

Week Three • Day Four

Ezra 4:6–24

I don't typically enjoy browsing through antiques stores, but I love treasures of my family history. My grandma made sure several items were preserved for her grandchildren, and many of them are in my possession. From the desk where I write, I can see one of those items—a decorative plastic container that holds her wedding rings. The two silver bands are the original rings from her wedding day in 1946 and are housed alongside a solid gold band my grandpa gave her years later when the other rings had become worn and thin.

Their love story is my very favorite, beginning with letters and cards mailed to each other during World War II. They had become pen pals while my grandpa was stationed in Germany with my grandma's cousin. The words penned to each other in casual conversation would soon blossom into deep affection for each other An old, tattered suitcase now houses these precious words, and within them unfolds a bit of our family history.

Written letters preserve stories from time past—an art that is somewhat lost in today's digital world of email and quick text messages. Letters were not prevalent in the Scriptures until Paul began to write his letters to the New Testament churches. But just like the first one we read from Jeremiah, the books of both Ezra and Nehemiah contain letters that help us understand the difficulties the exiles faced. Their history is preserved in ink on papyrus.

Today we will look at a letter sent to another ruler, King Artaxerxes. When placed above our narrative thus far in Ezra, we may become somewhat puzzled. Pay close attention as you read. We will take a moment to pull the details apart to clear up any confusion that there may be.

Read Ezra 4:6–24.

> » **Is there anything within this section of Scripture that is confusing to you? Jot it down, and hopefully your concerns will be answered in this lesson.**

» Don't skip this part; just take a second and think about it. You may find something different than I did. I'll give you a hint to what confused me. What are they currently building in Ezra 3:10 versus what the letter said they were building in Ezra 4:12?

I'm certainly not an expert in Persian history, so I had to do a bit of research to find out exactly what these letters were all about. What I discovered is this section appears to follow the sequence of the current events, but in actuality it does not. It's a parenthesis that moves us from a chronological account into a general description citing an example of the type of opposition that is taking place.[2] The example is found in Ezra 4:6–23, with verse 24 returning us to the current storyli ne.

As you reread the passage with this new understanding, fill in the blanks to the timeline these letters cover.

Read Ezra 4:4–5 that we covered in Day Three.

» 559–530 BC   King _____ of Persia

» 538 BC   The return of the exiles to Jerusalem

» 529–523 BC   Two kings not mentioned in the text

» 522–486 BC   King _____ of Persia

» 515 BC   The temple was completed

Read Ezra 4:6.

» 485–465 BC   King _____ (Xerxes of Esther)

Read Ezra 4:7.

» 465–424 BC   King _____

The people faced opposition the entire time of the rebuilding. This letter was recorded to give us a glimpse into the harassment they faced as they rebuilt the temple, the city, and later the city walls and gates under the leadership of Nehemiah.

Although we do not have the correspondence that was given during this conflict, these two letters give us an idea of the trouble the outsiders caused God's people.

Glance over the letter from Rehum, the officer in charge, written by his scribe, Shimshai, in verses 11–16.

» **What are the Jews accused of doing?**

» **What four reasons are stated within this letter that brought awareness to the danger of this building project against King Artaxerxes's reign?**

1. verse 12

2. verse 13

3. verse 14

4. verse 16

» **Do you think the accusations they were making were true? Why or why not?**

Read the following verses about each king of Judah to discover who they rebelled against.

» **King Hezekiah in 2 Kings 18:7.**

» **King Jehoiakim in 2 Kings 24:1.**

» **King Zedekiah in 2 Kings 24:20.**

» **Recall the response of King Artaxerxes of Persia in Ezra 4:17–22.**

» **What was discovered in the documents about Judah in Ezra 4:19–20?**

» **One example from the documents is found in 2 Kings 3:1, 7:8. How does this instance justify the king of Persia's fear?**

According to the Qere reading of the Hebrew text of 1 Kings 9:18, Solomon rebuilt Tadmor, the important oasis in the Syrian desert that controlled much of the Trans-Euphrates area. His international prestige is reflected in that he was given a pharaoh's daughter in marriage.[3]

» **What was the decree made by the king, and what reason did he give (Ezra 4:21-22)?**

The Jews did everything they had been accused of, and now were suffering the consequences. You may be thinking that it was a good thing to rebel against the enemy, but the roots of their rebellion went much deeper. They rebelled against God in the process.

Before they were taken captive, the sacrifices and festivals were celebrated in the temple, religiously. But that was the problem! The acts became simply that—religious traditions! The people of Judah coupled their sacrifices with the worship of the gods in foreign lands. They compromised their worship, and the result was captivity.

Now that they returned, they began to make choices that were hard, but good! The choice Zerubbabel made to refuse assistance from the men of the land was the inception of this turnaround for God's people. They could not take the chance of accepting help from those whose worship of God was paired with idols.

The result of their choice brought the opposition in full force to stop the progress of the temple. The same tactics were used on our exiles, even though the explanation in this letter is given from a different time frame.

Read Ezra 4:23.

» **What did Rehum and Shimshai and their associates do when they read the king's letter?**

» **What words are used to describe the tactic for stopping the rebuilding?**

» **Look up Ezra 4:23 in different versions. What other words are used to describe their tactics?**

Septuagint–the
Greek transla-
tion of the Old
Testament

» **The Septuagint adds the words "with horses and armed force." What effect would this have on the city?**

The destruction to the city of Jerusalem by the Persians described in the verses we just read was the reason for Nehemiah's visit to assist in the rebuilding.

Read Nehemiah 1:1–3 for this account.

» **How do the words of Hanani add to the overall picture of the destruction of the city?**

Verse 24 returns us to our current story line in Ezra. Read verse 24.

» **What was the result of the opposition?**

» **What year will the rebuilding continue again? Look back at our timeline we completed at the beginning of this lesson for assistance.**

» **Who will be the king of Persia when the exiles return to work?**

The work stopped! The whole reason the exiles returned to Jerusalem was to rebuild the temple. But when opposition struck, they left the house of the Lord unfinished.

The temple signified more than just a building—it signified worship. The worship of God was now laid to rest, and we find the city vacant of the worshipers.

Unleash the Power of Praise:

Reclaim the blessing of God found as we worship Him alone.

Have you ever started a project only to see it abandoned? It could be something simple like an afghan you began to crochet for a baby shower gift or a closet that was only partially organized. Oftentimes this unfinished work lacks any significance to our daily lives, but sometimes the projects left unfinished can be detrimental to the future.

What is something insignificant you have left unfinished?

What is something of value you have left undone?

There is great blessing when we complete a task given to us by the Father. It doesn't necessarily have to be something we create with our hands; oftentimes it's a work within the heart.

One of the greatest blessings in my life is time spent investing in others. As I write today, I have experienced this very thing. This morning in our worship service, a young man was baptized. My eyes filled with tears as his youth leaders told his story. His short journey on this earth has been difficult indeed. His mother died of a drug overdose, and he lives with his grandparents. The situation is far from ideal, as the relationship with his grandfather is volatile, but a Jesus-loving grandmother has brought him to church since he was little.

I was thankful to see the truth of the gospel realized in his heart at sixteen years of age when he made a profession of faith in Jesus. His baptism was celebrated as the cheers from our church family filled the building. They know his story, as children's leaders, junior high coaches, and now his youth pastor have poured truth into his life. It would have been easy to leave him alone since most of the time he saw adults as untrustworthy and, frankly, a hindrance to how he wanted to live. But these mentors and teachers did not give up. The work was hard and filled with obstacles, but they continued to love this young man. Today, even though his circumstances have not changed, he has a reason to live, and the evidence of rebuilding a life of worship is obvious.

As we think back to our exiles, opposition brought a halt to the rebuilding. What do you think will be the greater obstacle they must overcome to eventually re-build?

When the work God has asked you to do is interrupted, what is the obstacle that gets in your way?

There is so much blessing to reclaim as we come before God in surrender to the task He has for us to do. If there is something standing in the way of the work He has called you to do, relinquish it to Him. There is great victory to be found as we live each day in obedience to His calling on our lives.

Write a prayer of surrender to your God.

For we are his workmanship, created in Christ Jesus for good works, which God prepared before-hand, that we should walk in them.

EPHESIANS 2:10

Week Three • Day Five

Reflection and Application

They started well! The foundation for the temple was laid, and we heard our returned exiles worship together: "For he is good, for his steadfast love endures forever toward Israel" (Ezra 3:11).

They were thriving in the land of Judah until trouble arose! Fear swept over the nation, and they left the temple foundation undone to go home. The place of their worship was now abandoned along with their God.

Don't be too hard on our exiles. We probably would have picked up our hammer and gone home too. Fear does that to you! Sometimes it leaves us paralyzed, and other times it leaves us running for our lives—but it is something we must prepare for because opposition will come!

Do you remember on Day Three when we read about the lions attacking the foreigners because of their worship? Even after sending the Jewish priests to teach them proper worship, they still turned to other gods.

There was an intriguing command that was given three times at the end of that account. Read 2 Kings 17:35–39.

» **What was the command?**

» **Whom were they told to fear?**

The word *fear* in these verses is not the act of being afraid. It literally means to stand in awe of or in reverence.[4] How does that change your interpretation of these commands?

We worship an awesome and powerful God who is the only One worthy of our praise. It is He alone whom we should bow down to and worship with awe and reverence.

All too often we place people, success, material gain, and so much more at the forefront of our lives before God. Then when good things happen, we give glory to a person or an opportunity without crediting the living God, the giver of all good things.

» **What does Isaiah 42:8 tell us about God?**

In Galatians 1 we read about Paul as he tells the story of his life before and after his conversion. He states that he was literally unknown to the people to whom he was sharing the gospel, and within that honesty something glorious took place: "They glorified God because of me" (Galatians 1:24).

God was the One glorified, not Paul! This should also be our desire—that we become so completely unknown and unseen that it is God's glory on display. This is what happens when God is the only object of our worship. He gets the glory!

Worship happens when we replace being afraid of God to being in awe of Him. He doesn't want our lives to be centered around fear. Fear distorts our motives and leads to working to please God in an unhealthy way. God doesn't want our good deeds; He wants our adoration and devotion. He wants us to be so completely consumed by Him that nothing else matters, even when opposition comes.

Unleash the Power of Praise:

Reflect on what God is teaching you personally about our worship.

What is the foundation of your worship built upon? This may seem like an easy answer, but if you truly think about this, it might just become a bit more difficult as you proceed. It may help to answer some questions in specific areas of your life:

How do you spend your time?

What clutters your thoughts?

What words come from your mouth?

To what or to whom do you give your money?

What do you do when you receive good news? Bad news?

On whom do you depend for wisdom and strength?

What hinders your worship of God?

Pray through these questions and seek the Holy Spirit to guide you to truth as you answer. He may begin to guide you to questions that are not found on this page. When we are honest with the substance of our foundation, we can begin to rebuild our worship.

Worship that is centralized in God alone brings Him glory because:
>He is all we want.
>He is all we need.
>He is the One who can satisfy.
>He is the One to whom we stand in awe.

This is worship that flourishes and gives God alone the glory!

Meditate on Psalm 16:5–11 (GNT).

Mark it up below by making notations or comments regarding:
>What God has done for you specifically.
>How He has demonstrated His love and care for you.
>Why He is worthy of your worship.

Then pray through the psalm using your own words and experiences. This kind of prayer rebuilds the foundation of worship.

>You, Lord, are all I have, and you give me all I need;

my future is in your hands.

How wonderful are your gifts to me;

how good they are!

I praise the Lord, because he guides me,

and in the night my conscience warns me.

I am always aware of the Lord's presence;

he is near, and nothing can shake me.

And so I am thankful and glad,

and I feel completely secure,

because you protect me from the power of death.

I have served you faithfully,

and you will not abandon me to the world of the dead.

You will show me the path that leads to life;

your presence fills me with joy and brings me pleasure forever. (Psalm 16:5–11 GNT)

> *God is most glorified in us when we are most satisfied in Him.*
> —JOHN PIPER

REVIEW AND DISCUSSION

Day One

1. What changes have you experienced in a place where you have lived? What impact did this change have on the community?
2. Why was building the altar a priority to the exiles?
3. Read Hebrews 12:1–2. What is the race you are running in this season of life? What does it look like to run your current race in obedience within a life of worship?

Day Two

1. What was the age demographic of the returned exiles? What clues led you to this discovery?
2. When was the last time you saw God's people come together with one mind and the same love to complete a task? What was the result?
3. How did the people respond to the foundation of the temple being laid? How does their response show a misplaced heart of worship?

Day Three

1. How did the words of the enemy hinder the work to be done by the exiles?
2. What precautions can you take so that when the Enemy attacks you, you are not found alone and vulnerable to his assault?

Day Four

1. Do you have a story of a letter you or someone in your family received? What significance does it have in your life?
2. What was the result of the letter on the work the exiles were sent to accomplish?
3. What have you left undone in your life that had significant consequences?

Day Five

1. What does it mean to fear God?
2. What is the foundation of your life built upon? How does that affect your worship?
3. What is your takeaway for this week of study?

TEACHING NOTES

Rebuke

Week Four

WEEK FOUR • DAY ONE

Haggai 1:1–15

Last week we ended Ezra 4 with the work on the temple ceasing and the people leaving the city in fear. Even after the opposition settled down, the people did not return to the mission they were called to accomplish. God is about to send some visitors who will give us some insight into what they have been doing during this time.

This week we will take a break from the book of Ezra. As we study Haggai, one of the minor prophets, his message will give us a better understanding of the exiles and the time in which they lived.

The prophets are often overlooked in the study of God's Word. When is the last time you read through one of them except on your yearly Bible reading plan? And even then, the words may seem disconnected and the message difficult to comprehend. That's why we're going to take the time to dive in and study this message.

From Ezra 5:1 we discover two prophets who brought a word to God's people: "Now the prophets, Haggai and Zechariah the son of Iddo, prophesied to the Jews who were in Judah and Jerusalem, in the name of the God of Israel who was over them."

» **Which prophets brought a message to the exiles?**

One of the best ways to bring understanding to the text is to place it in the story line. If you were to read the books of Haggai and Zechariah without knowledge of Ezra's narrative, it wouldn't make much sense. You may be able to pull some basic truths from the message, but it only comes to life when layered over the story of the exiles.

Let's find out what the exiles have been doing for the past sixteen years as the temple still lay in rubble.

Read Haggai 1:1–6.

» To whom did Haggai the prophet give the message, and what were their roles in Jerusalem?

» What did the people say about rebuilding the temple?

» What did the people do instead of building the temple?

» What was the result of their efforts?

   » Their crops:

   » Their food:

   » Their drink:

   » Their clothes:

» **Their wages:**

On August 29, 520 BC,[5] the governor and high priest of Jerusalem were visited by Haggai, and he gave them a message. He began by recalling the state of the people of Jerusalem. They had left the task that was given them and spent their time working on their own houses and building their own lives.

The description used of their homes is quite significant. You see, Judah was built with stone. All the homes and buildings were constructed this way because trees were scarce. Even if you go to Jerusalem today, you will find a city made of stone. There are even government ordinances forbidding the use of wood because it is a limited commodity.

The wood delivered from the forests of Lebanon for the building of the temple took time and effort to even get to Jerusalem. Haggai's message informs us that God's people may have used the wood for the temple to build their own houses. Even with the threat of opposition gone, they continued to ignore God's instructions and build their own lives. We discover from Haggai their efforts brought no reward.

The problem they faced wasn't laziness. Building their own communities was hard work. The obstacle was displaced priorities. They desired the tangible things on this earth rather than the God who created it all. My husband always says, "Show me your checkbook (or what you spend your time doing), and I'll tell you where your heart is." It's not wrong to have or even want nice things, but it's prioritizing them over God that displaces our worship.

Haggai reminded them of the job they were called to do.

Read Haggai 1:7–13.

» **What is the first thing that the Lord of hosts told them to do?**

» **C_____ y_____ w_____**

» **If this instruction was given to you, what would be your answer? What have you been building for the past sixteen years?**

» **What did Haggai say would bring glory to the Lord?**

» **Why were their efforts in vain (v. 9)?**

» **By what means did God intercede to withhold abundance from their endeavors?**

» **We are not told that God's people were found worshiping foreign gods, but that their worship was sorely misplaced. What was the focus of their worship?**

This by no means implies that any time bad things happen in our lives it's because of misplaced worship, but it does remind us that when worship is displaced, we have a greater propensity toward sin. In our exiles' case, they had placed their worship on themselves and on their desires rather than on God. The everyday comfort of their lives became the hindrance standing in the way of the One who had called them to do a greater work.

What we know from Haggai is this: because of their disobedience, they did not prosper.

Sin ruins lives. I'm quite certain you will agree. It ruins the lives of those who are sinning, and it also affects all who are engaged with them. The exiles' disobedience led them to working hard with nothing to show for it, but God wouldn't let them waste their time much longer. There was work to be done, and it was their mission to complete it!

Read Haggai 1:12–15.

» **What was the first thing the people did in obedience to their God in verse 12?**

This action of their heart demonstrates they truly understood the gravity of their sin. It wasn't just about building the temple; it was about worship! Their first act of obedience was found in their repentance. Their sin was idolatry. It was not found in their wealth or even in how they chose to spend their time. Their sin was a heart issue and had to be remedied before the work could really begin—work that would not just rebuild the place of earthly worship, but would also restore their relationship with the Almighty.

» **What promise is given in verse 13?**

The exiles remembered this promise, and the Spirit began to stir in the leaders and the people. The building project was underway once again. We can look back at our story line in Ezra 5:2 to discover Ezra's record about their progress: "Then Zerubbabel the son of Shealtiel and Jeshua the son of Jozadak arose and began to rebuild the house of God that is in Jerusalem, and the prophets of God were with them, supporting them."

Sixteen years of stagnate faith was met with glorious worship when the work resumed. It's never too late to begin again. There are times in our life when we lose our focus and drift away, but God always draws us back to Him.

Unleash the Power of Praise:

Rediscover the meaning of worship.

In John 14, Jesus promises the gift of the Holy Spirit to indwell all those who believe. His role in our lives is included in verse 26: "But the Helper, the Holy Spirit, whom the Father will send in my name, he will teach you all things and bring to your remembrance all that I have said to you."

It is the Spirit who assists in bringing meaning to our worship. He is living in us to give us the power to worship properly in our everyday lives.

The Spirit is grieved when we have sin in our lives. Sin hinders our ability to worship God and give Him glory in all things.

At the beginning of this lesson, you were asked to consider your ways. What do your ways reveal about the placement of your worship?

Even good things can be sin and can hinder our relationship toward God. Reconsider your motives as you go about the daily ways of your life. When the motives of your heart align to the heart of the Father, that is proper worship.

One of my favorite encouragements from the Word is written by the prophet Jeremiah and helps me keep my motives rightly aligned. Take a moment to read these verses, using them as a springboard to check your motives and give your ways to the Lord through prayer: "Thus says the Lord: 'Let not the wise man boast in his wisdom, let not the mighty man boast in his might, let not the rich man boast in his riches, but let him who boasts boast in this, that he understands and knows me, that I am the Lord who practices steadfast love, justice, and righteousness in the earth. For in these things I delight, declares the Lord'" (Jeremiah 9:23–24).

> *Commit your way to the LORD; trust in him, and he will act.*
>
> PSALM 37:5

Week Four • Day Two

Haggai 2:1–9

I make decisions rather quickly, whether it's buying a shirt or purchasing a car. Sometimes those choices may get me in a bit of trouble, but for the most part they seem to just work out.

I have a dear friend whom I serve with, and she is the deliberator of all choices. Each year we devise a plan for our individual ministries, and it causes her so much headache. She often becomes paralyzed, worried that the plan she makes will fail.

One day she was working through her dilemma, listing everything she could do, along with all the reasons why it might fail. I finally turned to her and said, "Just do something. Anything! If you don't start with something, your ministry will just be stuck!"

That day she did it! She made the decision to begin Family Fun Nights for our church. In a matter of weeks, the families of our church were gathering together as never before, and with its success came a glorious affirmation from God, with our youth pastor and team of students stepping in to help.

Releasing her past failures and the lack of volunteers was key to her success in moving forward with something new. God blessed her obedience.

As we pick up with the exiles, they are still struggling as they trudge forward in their work. It seems they just can't release the past. In Haggai 2 we find the walls of the temple were being raised as Haggai brought another message to the people. It's now October 17th, just about four weeks from when the people had returned to their work.

Read Haggai 2:1–3.

Answer the questions that Haggai asked the people. Go back to Week Two, Day One to remind yourself of their responses to the foundations being laid.

» Who is left among you who saw this house in its former glory?

» **How do you see it now?**

» **Is it not as nothing in your eyes?**

The people of God were stuck! Once again, they came to a place of thinking more about the past than the future. The past is good for us to remember when we learn from it or when we reflect on God's faithfulness, but we should never want to return to the past. Remembering what God has done in the past gives us confidence of what He will do in the future. We can declare, "Look what God has done!" while moving toward the plans He has set before us.

» **What images are brought to mind as you read Isaiah 43:19?**

» **What could be the consequence for those who do not recognize that God is longing to do something new with them?**

Haggai questioned the people because he wanted them to reflect on their attitudes and actions. Until they recognized their need to move forward with the work God had given them and the roles they each played in the future of Judah, God's plan would not be accomplished. God didn't need them, but He chose to use them because He knew the blessings that would come with their obedience. He continued by giving the people a glorious promise.
Read Haggai 2:4–9.

» **What commands are found in verse 4?**

» **What was God's part in verse 4?**

» **What promises of the covenant still remained with the people?**

» **What promise was yet to come as the temple was completed?**

» **Why do you think this temple would have greater glory than the former temple built by Solomon?**

Even as I am writing, I am left undone in this glorious promise Haggai just ushered in with his words to the people. The glory that was still to come overwhelms my soul, and I hope you will feel the same as we discover Haggai's meaning.

Haggai gives the exiles a twofold prophecy in this portion of his message. The first would be revealed in five hundred years. This temple they were building would find itself dressed in gold as Herod began to reign. He found value in this place of worship, even though the manifested glory of God no longer resided within, as in the past.

The former temple was consumed in God's glory as the smoke of His presence hovered upon it. This symbol of His presence abandoned the temple upon its destruction by Babylon. Ezekiel prophesied of this day: "Then the glory of the Lord departed from over the threshold of the temple" (Ezekiel 10:18 NIV).

But now Haggai brought a message of hope of a greater glory that would surely come.

At the age of twelve, a boy would climb the steps with His parents when they came to Jerusalem for Passover. He would find Himself at home while amazing the religious leaders of the day with His knowledge of the kingdom of God. Although they failed to recognize it, the glory of God had filled the temple once again.

» **What does John tell us Jesus would bring to earth at His arrival in John 1:14?**

Jesus came to bring something to the world they never experienced—grace and truth. Even with His message of hope, the enemies of God would crucify His Son in the name of righteousness.

As Jesus cried out, "It is finished!" (John 19:30) and gave His life for the sins of the world, the temple encountered an amazing act as the veil was torn in two. This exposed the holy of holies for all to access, not just the Levitical priests. The glory of God would be available to anyone who would believe, giving direct access to commune with the Father. Jesus provides the way, and He intercedes for us until we are brought into His presence.

But this temple that saw the glory of God revealed to the world would not stand forever. Jesus Himself predicted its destruction several times as He walked this earth.

Read Mark 13:1–2.

» **What was the response of the disciples to the temple?**

» **How does their reaction to this building attest to their lack of understanding?**

» **What do you think their response will be to Jesus's prediction of this building they deemed sacred?**

The disciples had been walking with Jesus for almost three years, and they still didn't see it. Something greater than the temple had come, and He was among them.

We shouldn't be too hard on His followers, for we hold things that are temporal with great value as well. We cling to the things that will crumble instead of looking toward the steadfast rock of Jesus and the mission He has set before us.

» What are some things that we hold to in our religious practices that are temporal?

» Of these things, if they vanished, would they affect the mission of the church moving forward? How so?

The second prophecy seen in this passage is the future kingdom—the temple that will be built by the Lord Himself. On that day, though, the heavens, earth, and nations will shake and all things will fall apart, yet the temple will remain. Then all the people of the earth will come to worship the one true, living God.

Through Haggai, God reminded the people that they were building into something that they couldn't see. It may have looked like a shack to them, and it didn't look like the good old days of Solomon. They had no idea what was and is still to come. The majesty and glory of the Savior will one day reign from the very temple of God. On that day, everyone will worship Him alone! Glorious!

Unleash the Power of Praise:

Realize the challenge found in the misalignment of our worship of God.

The exiles continued to have the same struggles that had plagued their past, and they couldn't seem to move forward. Maybe this time they will make some progress, as a glorious promise outweighs their past remembrances.

What is in your past that paralyzes your moving forward? Is it an event, a person, or even your own shattered dreams? This question may be easy for some and more difficult for others. It may be something that you are not ready to acknowledge on paper.

If this is you, please take a moment to become quiet before God and allow Him to show you. The first step to moving into His glorious future is to recognize that which is holding you back. He will be with you on the journey. Do not fear.

We looked at Isaiah 43:19, which declared that God was doing a new thing. Read the verses surrounding this truth, and underline the words that express the newness God brings.

> Thus says the Lord,
> who makes a way in the sea,
> a path in the mighty waters,
> who brings forth chariot and horse,
> army and warrior;
> they lie down, they cannot rise,
> they are extinguished, quenched like a wick:
> "Remember not the former things,
> nor consider the things of old.
> Behold, I am doing a new thing;
> now it springs forth, do you not perceive it?
> I will make a way in the wilderness
> and rivers in the desert.
> The wild beasts will honor me,
> the jackals and the ostriches,
> for I give water in the wilderness,
> rivers in the desert,
> to give drink to my chosen people,
> the people whom I formed for myself
> that they might declare my praise. (Isaiah 43:16–21)

What was the result of this promise for God's people?

God desires to free you from the past that is holding you hostage. For some people, freedom can be as simple as taking it to God, releasing it, and moving forward.

For others, it may take much more work, which may require great forgiveness and counseling. Know that God will be with you on this journey.

Haggai brought some very important words to the exiles. How can these statements bring you to a place where you can declare God's praise and realign your worship?

Be strong.

Work.

I am with you.

My Spirit remains in your midst.

Fear not.

True and absolute freedom is only found in the presence of God.
—A. W. Tozer

WEEK FOUR • DAY THREE

Haggai 2:10–19

Two months have passed, and Haggai has entered the narrative once again to bring words of admonition and of blessing. The time stamp for this message is December 18, 520 BC. The prophet from God is about to address an issue, aiming directly at the heart. We find a call to holiness in his words.

Read Haggai 2:10–19.

» **Read verse 12 carefully and paraphrase the question using your own words.**

» **What was the answer the priests gave to this question?**

» **Read verse 13 carefully and paraphrase this question using your own words.**

» **What was the answer the priests gave to this question?**

As you paraphrased the above questions, I hope you found the simplicity given in the cultural example. The basic idea is this: holiness cannot be transferred, but unholiness can be.

When I was in high school, my preppy friends and I sought after the fad of the day: a pure white pair of Keds™. These simple tennis shoes were the envy of all who saw them. The problem was that their pure white condition soon faded. They were certain to find scuff marks and all kinds of dirt when exposed to my grimy high school campus. Four thousand teenagers sure can make a mess!

The pure white shoes did not make the dirt become clean, but the dirt sure did make those white shoes filthy. And this is Haggai's point found with his questions.

Holiness doesn't just happen by accident; holiness happens on purpose as we press into our worship of God.

Haggai takes a moment in his message to remind them of their past life before they commenced the building of the temple and to show them that their efforts to make a living had been in vain.

Read Haggai 2:15–19.

» **Paraphrase in one sentence the overall message of verses 15–17.**

All that happened to Israel in their past was in direct correlation to their disobedience. The trials they faced were not just a series of bad luck; they were the consequences of breaking the covenant as outlined in Deuteronomy 28.

This chapter in Deuteronomy begins with an *if/then* statement: "And if you faithfully obey the voice of the Lord your God. . . [then] all these blessings shall come upon you" (Deuteronomy 28:1–2).

Yet as it does in almost every case, the *if* statement is followed by a *but*: "But if you will not obey the voice of the Lord your God or be careful to do all his commandments and his statutes that I command you today, then all these curses shall come upon you and overtake you" (Deuteronomy 28:15).

The paragraphs that follow outline in detail the curses that came as a result of the broken covenant. The failure of their crops was not just the happenstance of mother nature. It was God fulfilling His promises to them.

Haggai reminded them of their past to give them a new hope of things to come. Their obedience was noticed, and God promised something grand!

» According to Haggai 2:18–19, what were the circumstances they had been facing, and what was God's glorious promise to them?

» What brought about this blessing?

The same people who had been found lacking would soon be found with abundance. Why? Because we serve a God of the second chance.

Unleash the Power of Praise:

Recognize the truths found in God's Word that encourage us to worship.

There are times when our efforts are centered on our lifestyles. We have little time to place God in our everyday work because it just seems so ordinary. The wheels keep spinning, but we never seem to get anywhere. In order to make a shift in this cycle, a right view of worship must be understood.

As I said at the beginning of the study, we are all created to worship. This is where the challenge begins. Properly aligned worship has its focus on God in all things, even the ordinary. Worship isn't just about our time at church, serving others, or even reading the Scriptures—worship is in our DNA.

Our worship doesn't stop when we pull out of the church parking lot on a Sunday morning. In fact, that's just the beginning. It's the placement of our hearts and attitudes within the natural rhythms of our life—as we do the dishes, read our children a story, interact with clients and coworkers, and talk with the store clerk and the dentist. Every interplay is met with the heart of the Father.

Proverbs 4:23 (NIV) gives this word of advice: "Above all else, guard your heart, for everything you do flows from it."

When we place this verse in context, we find the parent—most likely Solomon—giving a word of warning to his children.

> 20 My son, pay attention to what I say;
> turn your ear to my words.
> 21 Do not let them out of your sight,
> keep them within your heart;
> 22 for they are life to those who find them
> and health to one's whole body.
> 23 Above all else, guard your heart,
> for everything you do flows from it.
> 24 Keep your mouth free of perversity;
> keep corrupt talk far from your lips.
> 25 Let your eyes look straight ahead;
> fix your gaze directly before you.
> 26 Give careful thought to the paths for your feet
> and be steadfast in all your ways.
> 27 Do not turn to the right or the left;
> keep your foot from evil. (Proverbs 4:20–27 NIV)

In verses 20–22, what do we find is the key to guarding our hearts?

In verses 24–27, what are the instructions that will aid us in guarding our hearts?

We will look at this a bit more in depth on Day Five, but for now spend a few moments meditating on these words as you pray them to our Father. Jot down your thoughts as we continue this process of aligning our hearts of worship.

Give me words that offer hope filled with grace.

Give me eyes to see people as You see them.

Give me ears that guide my thoughts to hear their words with compassion.

Give me hands and feet that are compelled to meet their needs.

Give me a heart that reveals Your goodness within my actions.

Whoever believes in me, as the Scripture has said,
"Out of his heart will flow rivers of living water."
JOHN 7:38

WEEK FOUR • DAY FOUR

Haggai 2:20–23

Haggai took a step down from addressing the people and turned to give another message. This message was not to the entire congregation, but rather, it was to only one man, Zerubbabel. There was something unique about this man whom God chose to lead the people out of exile, for he was to become the next king of Judah from the line of David. But this was no longer his destiny, for the disobedience of God's people prevented this from happening. Still, God had an important role for Zerubbabel to play in Israel's history.

Read Haggai 2:20–22.

Haggai's message was one that brought hope to this throneless king as he gave Zerubbabel a glimpse into the future. He speaks of a time when the nations will be destroyed and God will reign victoriously.

> » **What action word is used in verse 21 to describe what will happen to the heavens and earth?**

Read Hebrews 12:25–29.

> » **What action takes place in verse 26 in this New Testament prophecy?**

> » **What do you think are the things that can be "shaken" in our world?**

» **What cannot be shaken according to verse 28?**

» **What is our response to the unshakable kingdom?**

» **What does this phrase tell you about God: "Our God is a consuming fire"?**

The God we worship is a God of grace and mercy who extends salvation to all who believe. Yet that same God is a God of wrath and justice. This is our God! We cannot have a loving God who is filled with compassion without believing Him to be a righteous and all-consuming holy fire!

The God who extended blessings to His people as they continued the work on the temple is the same One who is going to shake the heavens and earth and rid them of all evil.

The overall message is this: the nations will be shaken, but God's kingdom will remain—so keep on worshiping!

Zerubbabel did not live to see the dedication of the temple, for his name is not listed among those who attended, yet this magnificent promise spurred him toward living a life of worship.

In Jeremiah 22:24 we find God speaking to Zerubbabel's grandfather: "As I live, declares the Lord, though Coniah the son of Jehoiakim, king of Judah, were the signet ring on my right hand, yet I would tear you off."

After God removed the kingdom from his family line, Zerubbabel wondered how the honor would be given back to him. But God found him to be faithful and led the people back to a life of worship. In Haggai, the honor was returned to the line of David.

The signet ring would be figuratively placed back on his hand as he would look forward to an event that would happen four hundred years later—the birth of Jesus. Zerubbabel is found in the genealogy of Jesus in the book of Matthew. He sustained the line of David, which brought about the One who would rescue and redeem His people.

This rescuer would draw them away from their greatest enemy—themselves—offering eternal life.

Unleash the Power of Praise:

Reclaim the blessing of God found as we worship Him alone.

This promise brought hope that moved Zerubbabel to continue to lead the people toward a life of worshiping God alone, and his heart was moved to complete the task before him.

A similar promise is given in the New Testament to believers, bringing hope to those who are faithful to accomplish that which God has called them to do. This calling is found in the generosity of our time, our talents, and our treasures.

> Whoever sows sparingly will also reap sparingly, and whoever sows bountifully will also reap bountifully. Each one must give as he has decided in his heart, not reluctantly or under compulsion, for God loves a cheerful giver. And God is able to make all grace abound to you, so that having all sufficiency in all things at all times, you may abound in every good work. As it is written, "He has distributed freely, he has given to the poor; his righteousness endures forever." (2 Corinthians 9:6–9)

Read the blessing found in verse 8 in the NIV: "And God is able to bless you abundantly, so that in all things at all times, having all that you need, you will abound in every good work."

Using the verbiage of both versions, what three things are promised to you?
    1.

    2.

    3.

The context of blessing is found in our good works, which are seen through our generosity. Why is this true?

Do you have an example of generosity displayed to you that resulted in blessing the giver? Remember, generosity isn't just about money. There are many ways to live a generous life toward others.

Thank God for the ways you have experienced generosity in your life.

Thank Him for the blessing you have realized because of the obedience of your own generosity. Focus specifically on the three promises given in verse 8 and how they mobilize your daily worship.

We make a living by what we get, but we make a life by what we give.
—Winston Churchill

Reflection and Application

God longed to be the constant source of provision for the exiles, but first He had some work to do—not on the walls of the temple, but on the walls of their hearts. The words of Haggai's message reminded them that no matter how great the religious activity appeared to be, they needed to live a life of obedience rooted in holiness.

Haggai 2:14 reveals something only God could know about the exiles—the condition of their heart: "So is it with this people, and with this nation before me, declares the Lord, and so with every work of their hands. And what they offer there is unclean."

Here's the deal: they would not become holy because of their hands, but they would only become holy because of their hearts! The theology of our exiles got mixed up: *If I do this, then God will love me. If I work here, God will bless me.* It's a trap that we find ourselves caught in today.

The people looked for God's blessings, yet even in their perceived obedience, the crops seemed to fail. The people thought that it was their work that would bring God's blessings.

Unleash the Power of Praise:

Reflect on what God is teaching us personally about our worship.

There is a New Testament passage that brings about the beautiful promise of the gospel and our part in it:

> For the grace of God has appeared, bringing salvation for all people, training us to renounce ungodliness and worldly passions, and to live self-controlled, upright, and godly lives in the present age, wait-

ing for our blessed hope, the appearing of the glory of our great God and Savior Jesus Christ, who gave himself for us to redeem us from all lawlessness and to purify for himself a people for his own possession who are zealous for good works. (Titus 2:11–14)

These verses not only help us realize the source of our salvation, but also what sustains us in our sanctification.

What is the subject of verse 11?

What does that *grace* do?

It b_____ salvation AND t_____ us in how to live.

It's all about grace! We can stop trying to use our activity to get God's approval because God's love for us is not about our performance. He can't love us any more than He does, and He can't love us any less. He can only love perfectly because God is love.

And here's the beautiful thing about God's love-filled grace: it compels us to live in such a way that we want nothing more than to live godly lives that look forward to the blessed hope and glorious appearing of our great God and Savior.

Just as the words from Haggai encouraged the people to realign their hearts toward proper worship, so, too, do the words from the apostle Paul encourage us.

It is the truths from God's Word that encourage us to worship. These truths move our hearts from self-absorption to selfless adoration and point us to God alone as the source and sustainer of all that we are.

Write a prayer of thanksgiving below to God. Reflect on His character and on His

promise to carry you through each season of your life. Praise Him for His unfailing love that surrounds you as you rebuild your life of worship.

I do not at all understand the mystery of grace—only that it meets us where we are but does not leave us where it found us.

—ANNE LAMOTT

REVIEW AND DISCUSSION

Day One

1. Consider your ways! What have you been building the last sixteen years of your life?

2. What root problem caused the exiles to ignore the task God had called them to complete?

3. What promise did the exiles remember from Haggai 1:13, and what did it compel them to do?

Day Two

1. Are you a quick decision maker? How does that help or hinder the work God has asked you to do? What have you found to help in your decision-making process?

2. What was the twofold prophecy Haggai gave to the people, and what was its significance?

Day Three

1. Give an example of the truth that holiness cannot be transferred, but unholiness can be.

2. What is its meaning from the narrative of our exiles?

3. How can you guard your heart?

Day Four

1. What is the significance of Zerubbabel in the story line of Jesus?

2. What prophecy was given to Zerubbabel by Haggai?

Day Five

1. What is it that makes us holy—our hands or our hearts?

2. What is the difference between the work of our hands and that of our hearts? Why do we fall into the trap of doing instead of being?

3. What is your takeaway for this week of study?

TEACHING NOTES

_____

_____

_____

_____

_____

_____

_____

_____

_____

_____

_____

_____

_____

_____

_____

_____

_____

_____

Rejoice

Week Five

WEEK FIVE • DAY ONE

Ezra 5:1–5

In his book *Warfare Praying*, Mark I. Bubeck states, "The troubles in our personal lives, our churches, and in our world are due to a departure from the authority of the Bible as our only infallible standard of truth."[6]

In the book of Judges, we read over and over that "Everyone did what was right in his own eyes" (Judges 17:6). Those actions remained constant throughout history. When there is no foundation of truth, man determines within his own heart what is right and just.

Just take a look at what is happening in our world today, and we see the accuracy in Bubeck's statement, even though it was written more than sixty years ago. The search for truth has led our world to define this reality for themselves, leading to a standard that is far from the Word of God. This is found in our culture as it defines marriage, determines when life begins, and responds unbiblically when things don't go its way. When there is no basis for truth, chaos ensues.

Trouble has been in existence since Adam and Eve took a bite of the fruit, and it continues to prevail as man proceeds to "[exchange] the truth about God for a lie and [worship and serve] the creature rather than the Creator" (Romans 1:25).

The absence of this foundational truth in our culture stems from a loss of identity. Man does not recognize that he has been created in the image of God—*imago Dei*. We were created as image bearers of God. God is stamped on us, yet our world stamps out the very existence of God or creates God to be seen in the image of man! People create a "god in the box" of their own beliefs and desires.

Holding to truths God has given us is done by knowing the truth of God's Word, recognizing the truth of who we are, and doing the work He has called us to do.

As we enter into chapter 5 of Ezra, we will discover once again that the enemy has a plan to frustrate their progress. But this time something amazing happened—the people remembered the truth!

Let's join our exiles as we discover how the words of the prophets spurred them on to complete the task before them.

> Now the prophets, Haggai and Zechariah the son of Iddo,
> prophesied to the Jews who were in Judah and Jerusalem,
> in the name of the God of Israel who was over them. (Ezra 5:1)

Sixteen years had passed when God sent His prophets to encourage the people to get back to work.

Recall the events thus far by reading Haggai 1:3–8.

» **What did the message accuse the people of doing?**

» **What was the result toward their livelihood?**

» **What instructions from the Lord did Haggai bring to the people to encourage them to accomplish?**

> Then Zerubbabel the son of Shealtiel and Jeshua the son of Jozadak
> arose and began to rebuild the house of God that is in Jerusalem,
> and the prophets of God were with them, supporting them. (Ezra 5:2)

» **What did Zerubbabel and Jeshua do as a result of Haggai's message?**

» Who worked with them?

» Why is it significant that the prophets joined in the work of the temple? How did their cooperation in the rebuilding process benefit the people of God?

The direction was clear, and they went back to work! Wouldn't it be nice if God would give us clear direction? Oh, wait, I'm pretty sure He does. We will soon discover we have a similar mandate as the people of God in Ezra 5.

The exiles who returned were given the task of rebuilding the temple. This work was significant because the temple was more than just a building. The temple was the place God would dwell. Although God's presence would not descend upon the temple as in the days before the destruction, it was still the place where they would perform the sacrifices and meet with God. These offerings would enable them to interact with God while remembering His promises of a future kingdom filled with His glory.

The temple was a meaningful symbol to all who entered that God was indeed with His people. This completed building represented God's presence until the day when the promised Messiah came. His entrance into ministry would change everything.

» What did Jesus say would happen to the temple when He began His earthly ministry in John 2:19–22?

» To what was Jesus referring that the Jews failed to understand?

The temple was just a temporary house for the presence of the Lord. When Jesus came to the earth, He was the embodiment of God's glory. John 1:14 tells us, "And the Word became flesh and dwelt among us, and we have seen his glory, glory as of the only Son from the Father, full of grace and truth."

The tradition of meeting with God in the temple was no longer necessary because God incarnate was right before their eyes. Their refusal to believe that Jesus was who He proclaimed to be would lead the Jewish leaders to reject Him and crucify Him on the cross.

Three short years after His earthly ministry began, just as Jesus had prophesied, He rose from the dead and walked among them. When Jesus ascended to heaven, He had some very specific instructions for the disciples. These are God's instructions for us even today.

» **What was the mandate given to the disciples in Matthew 28:19–20?**

» **Does this apply to us?**

» **What is God's promise?**

The exiles built the temple with stones. Jesus is the chief cornerstone of the church. Believers are the living stones of the church today.

» **What does Peter say about God's view of the "living stones" in 1 Peter 2:4–5?**

» **What is God's design for these living stones?**

Our role in God's kingdom design is to be the bricks within the church. Believers are to cement themselves into the building up of God's church, following the commission given to us at Jesus's ascension. The construction of this building has great purpose as we build upon our brick by telling others the good news of the gospel. It's not about building a building—it's about building lives!

» **What is the danger in becoming a living stone as we live in the world, according to 1 Peter 2:4?**

We saw this very thing happening in Ezra as well.
Read Ezra 5:3–4.

» **What is the tone you perceive from the questions Tattenai and Shethar-bozenai asked the people who were rebuilding the temple?**

» **What happened the last time the people were faced with opposition (Ezra 4:24)?**

Read what happened this time when opposition came.
Read Ezra 5:5.

» **What was the result of the opposition this time?**

» **What reason is given for their continued work?**

» From what you know about the story thus far, what do you think made the difference?

If you skipped that last question, let's take a moment to think. If we long to be women changed by God's Word, we have to sit and soak in the tension that often exists. The tension is taking the black-and-white words found in the text and bringing in some color. The color is found in the emotions experienced or a shift in behavior. Their reaction to adversity was altered, and there must be a reason. This means answering the *why* question by taking in what we have already learned and applying those truths to offer application for our own lives.

Now as you reread this last question, take a moment to think about the experiences that our exiles had encountered thus far. The last time opposition arose, they stopped building for sixteen years, and their lives fell apart. What is different this time? What happened from the span of Ezra 4:24 to Ezra 5:5 that caused them to keep moving forward this time?

» What about you? Is there a time in your life when, due to circumstances beyond your control, you moved away from what God asked you to do? Now when the struggle comes, do you continue to be faithful? What has made the difference for you?

» Our exiles were people like you and me. Their struggle was equally as real as our struggles, yet they continued to do the work. Take a moment to rethink your answer to the question: What made the difference in the exiles' decision to continue rebuilding? It's this kind of hard thinking that makes the truth of God's Word root deep within you to bring long-lasting change!

You may have come up with some other ideas as to what made the difference, but my answer to the question is twofold:

1. They faced opposition before and learned from their past.
2. They had the prophets of God working alongside them.

They were not going to back down on the work God had given them to accomplish.

These people had faced opposition twice, both times while in the middle of the building project. The first time opposition came, they left their work for sixteen years, and not one time did the enemy come to harass them. The rebuilding resumed, and just like that, opposition arose again.

Any time God is doing a great work, we can expect opposition. The Enemy has no need to attack those who have already walked away in apathy from their faith, but when the building resumes, he is out in full force.

Unleash the Power of Praise:
Rediscover the meaning of worship.

As I am writing this study, our world is in the middle of a pandemic. The impact of this virus has paralyzed our people and threatened our nation. I never thought I would see the day when churches were being asked to close their doors, the gathering of God's people would be denied, and the worship of God's people would be silenced.

Yet the church has not allowed the building of God's kingdom to cease. The church has risen up against the oppressors to take a stand for truth. This is a moment that has challenged the focus of our worship, and we have found God to be faithful.

Believers all over the world have taken a stand for truth, using secular means for a sacred purpose. The gospel is being broadcast across the airwaves twenty-four hours a day, reaching people who have been blinded to its truth. The impact has been astronomical as lives are being transformed and destinies are changed.

Opposition will not stop the work of God's people. We have seen God's promises fulfilled throughout history, and we have the confidence He will continue to use His church until He returns. Paul wrote with certainty as he encouraged believers, saying, "And I am sure of this, that he who began a good work in you will bring it to completion at the day of Jesus Christ" (Philippians 1:6).

How can the church continue to prepare for opposition in today's world?

Do you have an example of a time when the church faced opposition from the outside during your lifetime?

Our engagement as bricks in the building of the church is crucial to the mission God has placed upon our lives. Although the mission does not change, the calling certainly looks different for each of us. So whether you are at home caring for small children, in an office doing finances, or volunteering in a shelter for victims of abuse, your life of worship shines for Jesus with confidence and courage.

Think about your calling in this season of your life. How can you build the church, brick upon brick, in this calling?

Petition Him today as you ask for the confidence and courage to live out your calling in the church, placing Jesus as the focus of your worship for all to see.

On this rock I will build my church, and the gates of hell
shall not prevail against it.
Matthew 16:18

WEEK FIVE • DAY TWO

Ezra 5:6–17

I recognize that fierce opposition will come against the church of Jesus Christ, and yet I wonder if I will have the courage to stand.

The accounts of believers being martyred for their faith frighten me, if I am going to be really honest with you. The headlines from countries around the world that oppose Christianity make me not only squirm, but also tremble.

I read the account of an Iranian man who converted to Christianity. Reverend Hossein Soodmand became an Iranian pastor and was arrested for apostasy. His arrest came with torture, and he was held in solitary confinement before he was sentenced to death. He was given the choice to see his family again if he would denounce his faith. He died alone, being hung and buried without his family knowing the dilemma that was before him as he courageously stood alone for Christ.

Before His death he wrote these words to friends who had fled Iran: "By following the example of the great shepherd of the flock, the Lord Jesus Christ, I am willing to sacrifice my life for my sheep. My escape from these dangers would weaken the flock of God and discourage them. I don't want to be a bad example to them, so I am ready to go to jail again and, if necessary, even to give my life for them."[7]

I'll only speak for myself, but as a woman who loves Jesus with everything I know, I am ill-equipped for such hostility. I am unsure I would stand for truth, and I might even become weak in the face of opposition. I like the comforts this life affords, and living in a self-absorbed culture does not help matters.

When these thoughts come to mind, my cry to God is this: *Help me love You more than I love my own life.* This is not an easy prayer for me as I see the foundation of truth in our world crumbling in churches all around the globe. Believers are seen as the enemy when adhering to the truth of God's Word. So when this adversity and persecution comes, I long to be found standing! "Therefore, take up the whole armor of God, that you may be able to withstand in the evil day, and having done all, to stand firm" (Ephesians 6:13).

As we review Haggai's message to the exiles, we find that the people who lived in the ancient world had the same struggles. When life got hard, they threw in the towel and left their work unfinished. But this time was going to be different. Haggai took the attention from themselves and spurred them on to complete the Lord's work—a work that was not easy, but in which they succeed this time.

Read Ezra 5:6–17.

» **What authority did Tattenai and Shethar-bozenai have in the land?**

» **What was the accusation they brought against the people of Judah?**

» **What was the response of the people of Judah, according to verse 11?**

» **What does this statement tell us about their work?**

» **Why does their answer appear more confident than the last time opposition had struck, according to Ezra 5:5?**

» As the Jews recall the events of their history, how do they show they are a people who have repented from the ways of their fathers?

» After stating the history of Judah, what did Tattenai and Shethar-bozenai suggest that the king should do?

The work on the temple moved forward even as opposition struck again. The answer the people gave in Ezra 5:11 was a statement of identity: "We are the servants of the God of heaven and earth, and we are rebuilding the house that was built many years ago." They knew who they were, and they knew the mission set before them. It was no longer a question, and it spurred them on to continue the work.

The answers given were words that brought glory to God alone. It's as if they said, "We really messed things up, but God has given us a second—well, maybe a third—chance. This time we are not going to stop—because we know our God is watching out for us. We are His people, and He has given us a job to do. So take what you have discovered to the king. God's got this!"

The confidence in their words came from a people who had been through this before. The first time they failed and walked away for sixteen years, but this time they chose to remember the promises of God, and the work continued.

Unleash the Power of Praise:

Realize the challenges found in the misalignment of our worship of God.

The word Haggai brought from God to their circumstance was the truth they needed to hear. This truth aligned their hearts to a place of choosing proper worship—worship focused on the work of God.

We, too, can learn from the truths found in God's Word, and this will lead us to worship Him. This worship is seen in Romans 12:1. This verse challenges us to crawl on the altar of surrender each day—surrender met with intentionality in our daily worship.

We are always worshiping, but the problem is some of us have really bad gods. The exiles spent sixteen years following after the god of self. Their houses, their families, and their crops were the focus of their daily lives. They found themselves in a state of constant worry, working hard with nothing to show for it. There is absolutely nothing wrong with providing for your family, but not at the expense of halting the work of God. When God is first, you will see His provision even when life gets hard.

Worry is often the cause of the misalignment of our hearts in worship. We find ourselves anxious about daily cares, and thus we justify our thoughts. When Jesus taught His disciples this concept in the Sermon on the Mount, He did so in a greater context. He gave instructions for them to live as citizens of the kingdom, serving only one Master, God the Father! Worry comes when we choose the wrong master and look to ourselves as the answer to our fate. Worry is a natural response in life when we encounter difficult times. It is our response to the worry that separates us from the world and reveals the alignment of a heart that worships God alone.

A life that trusts in the faithfulness of God, even when it is difficult, declares to the world that despite our circumstances, our God is unchanging and He will provide. This provision is seen in our daily material needs and in our spiritual needs to withstand opposition. Both cause us to worry, yet both can be met with the promises of God.

If there is something in your life that is causing you to worry, acknowledge it before God. Then pray the promises of His Word over your circumstance. Jesus said, "Here on earth you will have many trials and sorrows. But take heart, because I have overcome the world" (John 16:33 NLT).

Cry out to the Overcomer!

Therefore do not be anxious, saying, "What shall we eat?" or "What shall we drink?" or "What shall we wear?" For the Gentiles seek after all these things, and your heavenly Father knows that you need them all. But seek first the kingdom of God and his righteousness, and all these things will be added to you.

Matthew 6:31–33

WEEK FIVE • DAY THREE

We are the servants of [Cyrus the Great], and we are rebuilding the house that was built many years ago."

I hope you look at the statement above and see a huge fallacy from the written text. When we take a moment to think about the circumstance in which the Jews found themselves, the statement above may have given them the upper hand. Cyrus was the king who granted them permission to build and even gave them back all the artifacts for the temple. These words could have brought immediate resolution to the questions the governor brought to the people.

But God's people were not confused as to who it was that gave them the privilege to rebuild the temple. This courageous statement of identity found in chapter 5 pronounced their identity as it pointed toward the direction of the One whom they worshiped.

"We are the servants of the God of heaven and earth, and we are rebuilding the house that was built many years ago" (Ezra 5:11).

Their work continued as they awaited the response from King Darius. I wonder what the conversations consisted of each day as they met to build, knowing these king's associates were intent on seeing the building stopped.

> » **Give an example of a time when you have been found waiting for an answer. What is your typical response during the waiting?**

Waiting does not come easy for any of us. I remember asking God for wisdom in beginning the process of publishing a Bible study. I thought it would be an easy process, and I prayed for direction and doors to open. Doors did open, but they didn't look anything like I thought they would. The open doors led me to have a circle of experienced authors and teachers in my life before He brought the contract. He knew that this support system would be more beneficial than a published study. His timing is always best. In the time of waiting, I became more aware of my calling and His promise to fulfill it in my life. My purpose for this season of my life was affirmed by His gracious confirmation each step of the way. The placement of this life example within this study is the answer to my waiting.

Read the response of King Darius to his associates in Ezra 6:1–12.

Persian sovereigns would spend their winters in Babylon and the summers in Susa or Ecbatana.

> » **What was the direction given to Tattenai and Shethar-bozenai from King Darius (vv. 6–7)?**

> » **What do you think their response was when they heard the king's decree on behalf of the Jews?**

> » **Besides the building supplies needed for the temple, what else did Darius supply for the people (v. 9)?**

> » **What was the motive of the king as he provided the means for sacrifice (v. 10)?**

> » **What was the consequence for anyone who hindered the building of the temple (v. 11)?**

» **What do verses 10 and 12 tell us about Darius's view of the God of the Jews?**

» **Who was the source of help for the Jewish people as they continued to rebuild?**

The earthly means of help came from a pagan king, but the true source of help came from the Lord their God! We have seen God's hand throughout this story, as they were first granted permission from Cyrus the Great to return to Jerusalem. Then we see it again as Darius not only gave the permission to build, but also gave them all the resources they needed to build and to reestablish their sacrifices.

God's eye was upon them, and He would not allow His work to be thwarted. The prophet Zechariah reminded them of their place in God's care: "For he who touches you touches the apple of his eye" (Zechariah 2:8).

The same God who had His eye on the Jews while they carried out the work He had set before them also has His eye on us. We are part of the mission God has purposed to accomplish in the building of His church. There are times when the work will be hard and opposition will strike, but when we give ourselves to the work of the church, we can't lose. God's purpose will prevail, and His words will stand.

Unleash the Power of Praise:

Recognize the truth of God's Word that encourages us to worship.

The truth of God's Word guides us in the work of worship. We have a calling that is above any calling in this world—one that is ordained by God to carry out His work so the kingdom of God may be seen on earth.

How do you know you are doing God's work? Opposition will arise!

Opposition in our world is rising. More and more, the church is under attack as the world around deviates from the truth of God's Word. We are living in a Romans 1 scenario: "For although they knew God, they neither glorified him as God nor gave thanks to him, but their thinking became futile and their foolish hearts were darkened. Although they claimed to be wise, they became fools" (Romans 1:21–22 NIV).

Even though the powers of this world can be hostile to our faith, we must be able to recognize other forms of opposition to the work God has for us. Sometimes the greatest detriment to God's kingdom work is something we typically see as good: busyness.

There are times when we do our work for the kingdom, but at the same time find ourselves tired and running on empty. As women, our work often consists of caring for our families, serving in our church, managing our home, participating in our children's and grandchildren's schools, looking after our friends, making meals for the sick, and so much more. All these are good and admirable, but not to the expense of becoming weary and zapped of all strength.

As someone who lives a very busy life, I have had to work on giving out my best *yes* at the expense of saying a difficult *no*! I still have much work to do, but God is teaching me that when I say yes to what He is calling me to do, He will raise up the right person to serve in the places I surrender to Him.

Is there a subtle opposition in your life that distracts you from your calling? If you are unaware, ask God to reveal to you anything that may be in the way of you doing exactly what He has purposed for you.

The exiles were able to stay focused on rebuilding the temple once they remembered their identity: "We are the servants of the God of heaven and earth, and we are rebuilding the house that was built many years ago" (Ezra 5:11).

Your identity is not about what you do—it's about who you are.

Read through the list of our identities in Christ found in His Word, and thank Him that your identity is found in Him.

You are a new creation (2 Corinthians 5:17).

You are a chosen race and a royal priesthood (1 Peter 2:9).

You are His workmanship (Ephesians 2:10).

You are not condemned (Romans 8:1).

You are the light of the world (Matthew 5:14).

You are fearfully and wonderfully made (Psalm 139:14).

You are the temple of the living God (1 Corinthians 6:19).

In Christ Jesus you are a daughter of God through faith (Galatians 3:26).

*If we take our meaning in life from our family, our work, a cause,
or some achievement other than God, they enslave us.*
—Tim Keller

WEEK FIVE • DAY FOUR

Ezra 6:13–22

No work will prosper unless it is God's work built on His Word. Joshua 1:8 confirms this statement, as it reminds us, "This Book of the Law shall not depart from your mouth, but you shall meditate on it day and night, so that you may be careful to do according to all that is written in it. For then you will make your way prosperous, and then you will have good success."

As we conclude Ezra chapter 6, we see that God's people were indeed prosperous. They had been in Jerusalem approximately twenty-two years, and after working for almost six years, the temple was complete.

We will look at this last section and ask some diagnostic questions as we determine the who, what, how, and why of these passages.

Read Ezra 6:13–15.

The renewed work on the temple began on September 21, 520 BC, and concluded on March 12, 515 BC.

» **Discover the role each person had in this process.**

» **Who** *ordered*?

» **Who** *accomplished* **the order?**

» **Who** *prophesied*?

» **Who** *built*, *prospered*, **and** *finished*?

» **How was the work accomplished, according to Ezra 5:8?**

» Who ultimately gave the decree for the temple to be finished?

» Who were the secondary characters who gave the decree to complete the temple?

You may have wondered why the name Artaxerxes is present in this text. Although he did not have a part in the initial building of the temple, we will see him come on the scene in Ezra 7.

The completed temple stood in all its splendor, a glorious site to the weary exiles. Yet this temple had a very significant element missing—the ark of the covenant. The ark was lost during the Babylonian conquest. The holy place would appear different from the first as it was simply furnished with a table for the showbread, incense, and one menorah. We will find in the next section that even though the manifested presence of the Lord's glory would no longer abide in the temple, the people still found reason to rejoice.

Read Ezra 6:16–18.

» Who participated in the dedication of the temple?

> » the _____ of Israel, the _____ and the _____, and
> the rest of the _____ _____.

» What did they do at the dedication?

> » they c_____

> » they o_____

> » they s_____ the priests and Levites in their divisions

» Why did they complete these tasks (v. 18)?

» Compare the number of animals sacrificed at the new temple to those at Solomon's temple in 1 Kings 8:5, 63. Record what you find.

» What type of offering did the goats represent?

» How many goats were sacrificed?

» What did each goat symbolize?

» Why is this sin offering of twelve goats significant as the Jewish people began their new life of worship in the temple?

» What was the attitude of the people as they celebrated and offered sacrifices?

Worship was always the goal. When the people arrived back in the city of Jerusalem, the first thing they did was build the altar. Corporate worship happened. Then they got to work rebuilding the foundation, and eventually the temple itself. This process not only resulted in the place for the assembly to worship, but also instilled in them the practice of daily worship.

With the temple complete, their worship culminated as they celebrated two crucial feasts.

Read Ezra 6:19–22.

» **Which two feasts were celebrated by the returned exiles?**

» **According to verse 21, who else joined in the feasts?**

When Zerubbabel began building the temple foundation, the people of the land came to help. He refused their assistance, which made the people angry. Here we find the same people of the land celebrating with them. Some are from gentile nations and others are the Jews taken captive by Assyria; they would become known as the Samaritans.

The Samaritan people came into existence two hundred years before this event when Assyria captured Israel. They forced the Jews who were left in the land to interbreed with the foreign nations. During this time, this mixed race of the Jewish people resided in the land and observed the people of God rebuilding the temple. We know from accounts in the New Testament that Samaritans were despised by the Jews. A Jewish person would not even walk through their city. It wasn't until the encounter with the woman at the well that we find the hope of restoration coming to them once again through Jesus Himself (John 4).

The Samaritan people must have noticed the dedication of the exiles, which screamed a testimony of God's mercy. This led them to participate in the purification ceremony to grant them a seat at the table.

They celebrated together for two reasons. First, the temple was complete and worship could resume without hindrance. Second, they had a newfound unity. God was moving among them, and they were led to joy-filled worship together with all the people of the land.

Unleash the Power of Praise:

Reclaim the blessing of God found as we worship Him alone.

The word *joy* used in this passage is found in only two other places in Scripture. It is the Hebrew word *hedwah* found in 1 Chronicles 16:27 and Nehemiah 8:10.

Read 1 Chronicles 16:27 and Nehemiah 8:10.

What attribute accompanies joy in each of these verses?

How does this additional attribute accentuate the joy that was expressed in their worship?

Recall a time that you completed a task or found great success in something God called you to do. What were the emotions of your soul?

The joy that overcomes my soul during success is often expressed in tears. I have had the privilege of leading many events that, after many months of work, culminate in the gathering of people. My favorite memory in my early years of ministry on our church staff was of leading a children's choir each summer. The overwhelming emotion of joy filled my soul as the overture would begin and the children would take their place on stage, their voices filling the room.

The work was overwhelming and challenging at times, as each child's personality brought obstacles that affected the whole. But great reward and joy came when each child was moving in sync and proclaiming the truths they had learned through song.

Joy was not possible, though, without the Lord's enduring strength. Great joy comes as a result when the work is hard. Do you agree? When success comes easy, it is met with relief, but when it has been accomplished through blood, sweat, and tears, the outcome seems more like a victory.

It is then you look back and recognize that God had you all along the way. His gentle whisper in moments of desperation would say, "This is the way, walk in it" (Isaiah 30:21). Your obedience to His call is found in the blessing of His success in you.

God uses us to accomplish His will, and when we act in obedience, this is our worship!

Thank God today for the successes He has allowed you to realize. Thank Him for His Word that guides you to discover truth. It is only because of Him that we can prosper.

For then you will make your way prosperous, and then you will have good success.

JOSHUA 1:8

For more information on *Jewish Feasts*, go to caroltetzlaff.com and click on "Ezra Study."

WEEK FIVE • DAY FIVE

Reflection and Application

Our exiles experienced tantamount highs and tumultuous lows, yet both led them to find joy.

What brought the shift in their worship as they reset their focus on the work God had for them? It was His Word!

Haggai and Zechariah brought words of encouragement and exhortation from the Lord with much enthusiasm. These words shifted their focus back to the task at hand and reoriented their worship.

Their work on the temple flowed from a heart that remembered God's calling, reclaimed God's promises, and revealed their identity—even in the face of opposition.

The statement of this assurance is made clear in Ezra 5:11: "We are the servants of the God of heaven and earth, and we are rebuilding."

God's view of them did not become greater as they obeyed—they were God's chosen people all along. What shifted was their understanding of this view.

Their obedience brought them to a place where they could not be stopped no matter what obstacles stood in their way. They knew they were servants of God, and they had been called to accomplish something for a greater purpose.

» **Have you ever fallen into the trap of performance as you work toward pleasing God to obtain His favor?**

» **What is the outcome of work done with this motive in mind?**

» **What reminders can you put in place that will help you recognize God's view of you?**

Unleash the Power of Praise:

Reflect on what God is teaching you personally about our worship.

Be reminded of your identity in Christ. Oh, daughter of the King, you are loved by the One who gave you His beautiful gift of grace founded in Jesus. His grace not only gives you salvation, but also provides daily sustenance for every aspect of your life. May the truths that you have found lead you to a life of delightful and magnificent worship of the One who is so worthy!

Write a prayer or your thoughts below as you recall your identity and what it means to you in this particular season of life. Use the certainty found in the statement of the exiles in Ezra 5:11 and make it true to you:

"I am a servant of the Most High God, and I am rebuilding."

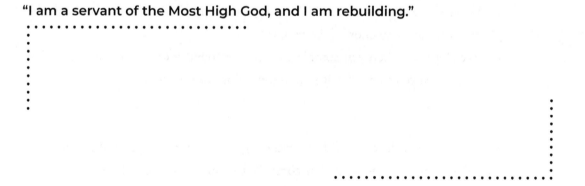

Taste and see that the Lord is good; blessed is the one who takes refuge in him.

Psalm 34:8 (NIV)

Review and Discussion

Day One

1. How is truth defined in our world? What impact does this have on our culture?

2. How can we have a foundation based on God's truth?

3. What is your role as a brick in the building of God's church?

Day Two

1. Do you see hostility in the world against believers? What is your response to this tension as it comes to your home and church?

2. Worry is a natural response to the circumstances of our lives. If it is our response to worry that sets us apart from the unbelieving world, what is the reality of that response?

Day Three

1. What is your response when you are found waiting for answers?

2. How do you know God is at work in the church and in our world? Why? How can you prepare yourself to continue the work?

3. What is a subtle opposition in your life that distracts you from God's calling?

Day Four

1. What is the significance of inviting the people in the land to rejoice with the exiles at the completion of the temple?

2. Recall a time when you completed a task or found great success in something God called you to do. What were the emotions of your soul?

Day Five

1. God's view of the exiles did not become greater as they obeyed Him. What was the shift in their mindset that compelled them to complete the task God had given them?

2. What truths can you claim in your identity in Christ that lead you to obedience?

3. What is your takeaway for this week of study?

TEACHING NOTES

Reform

Week Six

WEEK SIX • DAY ONE

Ezra 7:1–10

"This Ezra went up from Babylonia. He was a scribe skilled in the Law of Moses that the Lord, the God of Israel, had given, and the king granted him all that he asked, for the hand of the Lord his God was on him." (Ezra 7:6)

The story of my life is one in which I can look back and say, "The hand of the Lord was upon me." The circumstance of my life, from the moment I was conceived, had the opportunity for great disaster, but the hand of the Lord was upon me. Looking back over my life, I see His protection and guidance from infancy to adulthood.

At the age of ten, I moved into a new house with my family—my mom, grandparents, and little brother. Our neighborhood was brimming with kids. Not long after our move, I began to assist a young mom as she cared for her three boys. What began by simply playing with them while she was home turned into full-time babysitting for many years while she went to school to become a teacher. After she graduated, they moved away, and I lost all contact with them. But God's hand was upon me, even in those years of watching kids. Many years later, after I graduated from college with a BA in elementary education, I received a phone call from her. She was now a principal, and her connections landed me my first teaching job in a very sought-after school district. I thought I was simply watching the neighborhood kids, but God had a greater plan in mind, as I know His hand was upon me.

Our study has brought us to the chapter in Ezra that launched my deep affection for this book. I resonate with the assurance Ezra found as he obeyed God's calling. Three times in this chapter we will read, "the hand of the Lord was upon him." The security found in this statement brings much more than a simple care and concern for the happenings in Ezra's world by the divine Creator; it brings about the beauty found in God's sovereignty.

The first time I read this chapter in Ezra, my image of this man changed from the flannel-graph portrait of an old man with a long, white beard in regal robes to a young, handsome man eager to learn everything he could about God's people as he scoured the ancient scrolls for truth. Born during the exile in Babylon, his own personal study led him to follow the task God had prepared for him.

Let's rejoin the story of our exiles and discover how the namesake of this book entered the narrative.

We ended Ezra chapter 6 with the people in joyful celebration! The temple was rebuilt, the feasts had been reestablished, and worship had been restored. All seemed well in the land of Judah as God's people realigned their hearts in obedience and service to their God.

As the clock ticked onward, so did their lives. When chapter 7 opens, we find the words, "Now after this . . ." It appears at first glance that it could be the next day, but in actuality, it was sixty years later. Much can happen in sixty years, as the generations morph one into another. Although we won't see the full scope of their circumstance until next week, we find that God was already working, as He raised up someone to build something new. But this time, the rebuilding took place in their hearts.

Read Ezra 7:1–10.

Welcome, Ezra! It's about time he appears on the scene. Have you been wondering where he has been? He's been living in Babylon among the other Jews who were born there.

Ezra arrived with an ancestry that could not be denied. His genealogy found in his introduction spanned sixteen generations. This is quite a unique list compared to the other characters found within the Old Testament.

> » **What role did each of the men in Ezra's genealogy play in Israel's history? If you are unfamiliar with the names, see verse 5 for a clue.**

> » **Why was his family lineup so crucial to the role he would play in Israel's history? If you need some help with your answer, recall Ezra 2:59, 62.**

> » **What was Ezra's skill that was given to him by the Lord in verse 6?**

"Teacher" is the Old Testament form of rabbi. Ezra was a man who studied and taught the Scripture. He was able to interpret the law and instruct the Jews on how they should live according to it.

Ezra believed he was well prepared for the journey from Babylonia to Jerusalem. Joining him on this trip was the second wave of exiles whom the Spirit stirred to return with him. It had been well over one hundred years since the exiles were taken to Babylon, which means none of these people would have ever even been to Jerusalem. His trip began on April 8, 458 BC, and they arrived in Jerusalem on August 4, 458 BC—a 119-day trip. There was certainty that they would arrive, but their journey was not without complications.

We will learn more about this trip tomorrow as our narrative returns us to his travels, but for now we will focus on the man, Ezra.

We can find out much about this man of God within the text, along with why God chose to use him. Not only was he well learned in the Law of the Lord, but he was seen as a man with status within the political climate of Babylon. All Ezra knew about God's people was what he had learned from the ancient writings and from the teachings of his father. He was a priest without a temple. Nevertheless, God was raising him up to become the one who would lead the Jews to repent of their sin.

» **What three things does verse 10 tell us about Ezra?**

» _____ his heart to _____ the _____ of the Lord,

» to _____ _____,

» to _____ his _____ and _____ in Israel.

» **Where does the verse say he was going to teach?**

It was God who set this path in Ezra's heart. Can you imagine young Ezra reading about the origin of his people, hearing the stories of the conquest of the promised land and the history of the kings, while all the time longing to be a part of the story? God had placed that desire in his heart, and Ezra was doing all that was necessary to see that he fulfilled God's purpose.

» There is a phrase that is given twice in this short passage we are studying today. Read back through it, and write down what you discover from verses 6 and 9.

» How would you describe this phrase in your own words?

God's gracious favor was upon Ezra. God was there to give him everything he needed to accomplish the task at hand, but it didn't begin when Ezra appeared on the scene—the work began years before. Ezra's practices in his past were what led God to choose him.

As Ezra began to study, his heart must have been stirred toward his own people, the Jews. He may have heard of the struggles his people were having in the land and prayed for them. One of his requests could have possibly been that God would raise someone up to teach and instruct the people in righteousness. If so, I wonder when he began to understand that he was the very answer to his prayers.

The call was on his life, and he was prepared to answer. His years of study gave him a vast knowledge of the law. He could articulate what God was asking His people to do and why it was so important. He was a teacher of the law, and that qualified him for the task God prepared for him, but what added greatly to his ability was the fact that he didn't just know the law—he also obeyed it.

Teachers are much more effective when they live out what they are teaching. Ezra's life must have been a shining example of God's truth in the community of Babylon because four thousand more people rose up and returned with him to Jerusalem. These were people who had to be very intentional to learn about their heritage and what God had done. They had no exposure to sacrifices, feasts, and temple worship, yet they felt the call to return with Ezra. It wasn't a vacation; it was a complete shift in everything they held dear, and they were still willing to go.

The nine-hundred-mile journey lay before them. While the people sold their homes and packed their bags, Ezra prepared to go before the king. Permission to return was just part of the request, for the people needed provisions along the way.

Unleash the Power of Praise:

Rediscover the meaning of worship.

In Psalm 139:10 we read of God's ever presence with us. The psalmist reminds the reader that wherever they may be, "even there your hand shall lead me, and your right hand shall hold me." The promise given is that God's hand is upon us.

Paul's teaching to the people in Ephesus reminds us that we are created to do the good works God has for us, and that these works were planned even before we were born (Ephesians 2:10). When we understand the beauty in this truth, our work is covered by the very hand of God, and we can rest in His purpose for us.

By *rest*, I don't mean to be still. We rest because we are certain that God will accomplish His purpose within us. But we can't just sit around and wait for it to happen. Like Ezra, we are always in the state of preparation, and this defines our daily worship.

What three things did Ezra do to prepare for the task God had for him (v. 10)?

How are those three things being manifested in your life?

Which areas are easy and in which areas do you struggle?

God has something just for you to accomplish. What does 1 Peter 5:6 say about the timing of this task?

How have you served God in the past and in the present?

Is God stirring your heart to lead you to something new in obedience to Him? Where is He leading you?

Ezra found success because the hand of the Lord was upon him. Even though he came from a line of righteous priests, it was not his legacy that gave him credentials to lead—it was his God! Regardless of your past, God can use you to build His kingdom.

Study, obey, and be ready to move in the proper time when the call comes! This is a glorious act of worship.

God wants to do a deep work in us before He can do a deep work through us.
—CHRISTINE CAINE

Week Six • Day Two

Ezra 7:11–28

I love the details. I want to know everything from the landscape of the setting to the emotions that drive each character.

Last Easter I found myself wondering about the everyday people who encountered the crucifixion. My thoughts led me to imagine the reaction of an everyday priest as he entered the temple the next day. Such a character is not found in the text, but my soul longs to know the ordinary people not mentioned throughout the pages of the narrative.

My curious thoughts led me to write a short story entitled "Torn." This short story embraced the life of a priest as he entered the temple to find the veil torn and the holy of holies exposed. My imagination wandered through the temple as he found himself overwhelmed with emotion. The story I wrote demonstrates my yearning to know more about the characters surrounding the narrative of Scripture and the narrative itself. The story can be found at caroltetzlaff.com in the Ezra resource tab.

From the beginning of time, we read of a garden, but life in the garden is silent. We read of the birth of our Savior, but the stable happenings regarding the entrance of Immanuel are missing. I don't just want to assume or speculate; I want to know details!

What did everyday life look like as Adam and Eve lived in glorious perfection? I imagine them spending their days sitting on a blanket of soft grass while leaning back on the velvety fur of a lion resting beside them. When hunger strikes, Eve would find sustenance in the lush garden filled with plump vegetables ready for picking. Adam may have hollowed out a few coconuts to use for their beverage of choice, which would have been the milk from a cow or juice from the fruit found on the citrus trees. Sitting beside a flowing river, they would eat these delicacies while awaiting their daily visit from their Creator. What did they talk about? Oh, to know the depth of conversations that occurred between humanity and the almighty God! How long did it take before the serpent appeared and all was lost? This garden story, along with so many others, leaves me wanting more.

Today we are given some details into Ezra's travel from Babylon to Jerusalem. This account gives us a glimpse of what the commute entailed. This story line allows us to feel the emotions of the one in charge of the endeavor and the responsibility he endured for the people he was leading.

Ezra's journey begins with a letter that Artaxerxes, the king of Persia, wrote. Read Ezra 7:11–26.

» **What are we told that the king gave to Ezra from earlier in our chapter—Ezra 7:6?**

» **As we read the letter King Artaxerxes wrote, we are able to discover the requests that Ezra made of the king. Make a list of the all the things that Ezra could have requested.**

The requests fulfilled by the king can be categorized in three statements:

    The gathering of people

    The giving of offerings

    The governing of the land

Ezra was a man of courage and determination. This Jewish exile approached the king with boldness as he made his requests. There was no doubt he recognized God's hand upon him as he entered the king's presence. The king was ready to listen and acted favorably. We see throughout the letter that Artaxerxes acknowledged that the God of Ezra was in a position of authority, even over his own.

» **How many times does King Artaxerxes refer to Ezra's God?**

» **In verses 12, 21, and 23, where does he acknowledge the residence of Ezra's God to be?**

» What did this residency say about God's authority in the king's mind?

» What pronouns did Artaxerxes use that affirmed he was not a follower of Ezra's God?

» What instruction was given to the people of the land in which Ezra would travel (vv. 21–24)?

» What instruction did Artaxerxes give to Ezra about the law of God and the submission of the people to it (vv. 25–26)?

» If you were getting ready to travel nine hundred miles to Jerusalem, how would the king's letter make you feel?

The gracious provision of our God to this second band of exiles as they were about to embark on this mission is astonishing. I don't know about you, but when I read the words of this pagan king, I am in awe. God provided once again more than the people could have expected. He showed them His favor with overwhelming abundance.

Can you even imagine what Ezra was thinking as he unrolled the scroll and began to read? His response was a prayer of worship, for his requests had been met with great fortune. His prayer uttered obvious amazement over the provision of his God.

Read Ezra 7:27–28.

» To whom was the credit given?

» What do you think Ezra did to assure the men of Israel that God was in this plan?

» Why would this give them confidence to leave everything they knew and follow Ezra to Jerusalem?

Ezra overcame his fears and saw God do a mighty work in the heart of the king, his counselors, and his officers. It was God who led Ezra, for His hand was upon him.

Unleash the Power of Praise:

Realize the challenges found in the misalignment of our worship of God.

Ezra was preparing the people to walk the long road back to Jerusalem, recognizing that God was leading the way.

Ezra brought together the men and their families from Babylon's exile to travel in freedom to Jerusalem with great confidence. God was with them, so how could there be any doubt?

At first the people may have thought Ezra was crazy for leaving the comforts of home to travel for three months to a land they didn't know. But God would not let them dwell in their doubt as He moved the heart of the king to usher in a way. The words from the king gave the people the assurance God was in this. God carved out a path so very clear they could not miss it.

Ezra was given clear direction for his next step, but oftentimes in our lives we are left wondering. *Which school should I attend? Who should I marry? What job is right for me? Where does God want me to live? How can I best serve Him?* These types of questions plague our minds as we venture through life.

I'm going to give you the answer to these questions for both your life and mine. Every decision we make is of God if it is met in obedience through properly aligned worship in accordance to His Word.

Sometimes the way seems so obvious, but other times we wonder. Yet this I know to be true: "The Lord makes firm the steps of the one who delights in him; though he may stumble, he will not fall, for the Lord upholds him with his hand" (Psalm 37:23–24 NIV).

Delighting in the Lord is found in our worship of Him. It encompasses everything from our acknowledgment of His character to the realization of our identity. This drives us into a life of obedience. Whether we are at home taking care of the kids with our days filled with cooking, cleaning, and laundry, or we are the CEO of a billion-dollar corporation with our days filled with meetings and mergers, God wants us to surrender to Him and find our contentment in Him.

We may falter along the way and at times stagger to take another step, but God is there. He is ready to catch us before we fall. That's the promise given by the psalmist. Not only does He hold our hands, but He also has a tight grip on our hearts so that the choices we make will find us standing firmly in His will.

Is there something in your life about which you are uncertain? What are the choices before you at this moment?

What does obedience look like in the above circumstance?

What fears do you have about making the "wrong" choice?

What must you do to trust God in this decision?

Take some time to pray and give your current choices to God. Pray through the promises you know to be true regarding your circumstances. Then trust that the decision you make will be blessed because in it you are found worshiping with surrendered obedience. Dear child of the King, the hand of the Lord is upon you!

In your hand are power and might,
and in your hand it is to make great and to give strength to all.

1 CHRONICLES 29:12

For more information on *Levites and Ezra's Geneology,* go to caroltetzlaff.com and click on "Ezra Study."

WEEK SIX • DAY THREE

Ezra 8:1–20

I mentioned earlier that our world is living through a pandemic that has shut down our country. For the first time in my life, the doors of the church were locked and we were forced to come up with an alternative to our traditional gathering. This did not just affect the weekend worship services, but it affected every aspect of ministry.

Within a week, the church where I serve was transformed to a fully online congregation, serving the people God had entrusted to us. Our weekly women's Bible study was now ZOOMing into homes as we gathered on the screen.

As I look back at that time, I am so grateful for the team of women God placed around me. These women did what was necessary to see that each of their groups stayed connected to each other and to the Word.

Choosing the right people for your team is critical to the growth of any ministry. Oftentimes you don't even know they are the right people until crisis strikes. Ezra faced crisis as he prepared to travel to Jerusalem. The men he chose aided him in finding success when a situation was brought to their attention that left them paralyzed.

Ezra chapter 7 ends with the words, "I gathered leading men from Israel to go up with me."

Ezra was on the hunt for people to join him in his mission. Ezra was a man with vision. He was given a big assignment from God and knew he would need help to see it accomplished. The first assistance came from the king, but now he needed a group of people to join him.

Ezra chapter 8 contains another list of exiles who were willing to go to Jerusalem and be a part of Ezra's plan. Most of the people listed were from families who had gone before them, the group of exiles who returned with Zerubbabel. Although the move would be difficult, it would end with a familial tie that would spur them to continue the journey.

Read Ezra 8:1–14.

There were just over fifteen hundred men who joined Ezra, along with women and children. Their journey was the same as those who had gone before. It took about four months for this nine-hundred-mile trek.

A few days into the journey, Ezra made a realization that halted their travel.
Read Ezra 8:15.

» **What did Ezra realize as they began their journey to Jerusalem?**

» **Why was this an issue?**

The role of the Levitical priests during these ancient times was crucial to the work of the temple. Ezra recognized that the real work he was sent to do could not be accomplished without these men to assist him in the task. It was more than just rounding up people with Levitical ancestry, for even though all priests were Levites, not all Levites were priests. One example from history is the priest Zechariah in Luke 1. This priest had a son named John who is found in the New Testament narrative. We know him as John the Baptist, the forerunner to Jesus. John was born a Levite, yet he was not called to be a priest. John's role was that of prophet, proclaiming the coming of the Messiah.

Ezra knew he could not return without the assistance of the Levitical priests and temple servants, so he devised a plan.
Read Ezra 8:16–20.

» **What description does Ezra use for the men whom he sent to Casiphia?**

» **Why was this trait important to the task at hand?**

» To whom did they give the credit for their successful mission?

» How many more people joined Ezra in the journey to Jerusalem?

Ezra may have been discouraged at the number of people who had chosen to join him to do God's work in Jerusalem. There were many Jews who decided life in Babylon was better. They had homes and work that made life comfortable, even in a pagan culture away from the worship of God. But those who followed the call to return would see God move in a mighty way.

Unleash the Power of Praise:

Recognize the truth found in God's Word that encourages us to worship.

Giving up our comfortable life to follow Jesus is a struggle many find themselves in today. Jesus gave us an example of this when He walked the earth. Although some would accompany Jesus on His mission, many others were not willing to give up everything to follow after the Messiah.

From Luke 9:57–62, what are the three reasons Jesus gives that demonstrate the sacrifice found in following Him?

Following Jesus does cost us something. We may not understand the full weight of that statement in our lives, but there are many people who do. For us, it may be the sacrifice of time, relationships, or money, but in many parts of the world, people are called to give their very lives. They know that saying yes to Jesus could cause them to be shunned from family, from their work, and even from the only place they know to be home. Others risk their lives to take the gospel to places that are hostile toward the truth.

Do you have an example of a story or someone you have known who has sacrificed much for the gospel? Jot it down below so you can share it with your group.

The encounter in Luke 9 with those who chose not to follow Jesus is followed by Jesus making a request of His disciples. Luke 10:2 tells us, "And [Jesus] said to [the disciples + the seventy-two who had chosen to follow Him], 'The harvest is plentiful, but the laborers are few. Therefore pray earnestly to the Lord of the harvest to send out laborers into his harvest.'"

Our world is not much different than it was in the first century. Jesus sees a world that is in desperate need of the truth He had come to reveal. In Luke 10, He gives His followers supernatural gifts and tells them to go and use these gifts to show people the truth. They go and do extraordinary things. When they return, their excitement is uncontainable:"Lord, even the demons are subject to us in your name!" (Luke 10:17).

As Jesus sent them, His mission was not to send a traveling show of miracle workers to wow the crowds. The desired outcome was more laborers—more people who would not just marvel over the miracle but who would also be changed and follow after Jesus! He wanted followers who would take His truth to the world.

That is still Jesus's plea today. He wants people like you and me to follow after Him and bring the truth from the Word to expand the kingdom. He is pursuing people who live a life of worship, following after their King.

Take a moment to evaluate your own life and your service to Jesus. Are you faithful to His calling? Are you one of His laborers?

Thank Him for the opportunities He has given you to serve Him, and then ask Him to continue to lead you in His way.

*Submit to His authority and He will guide your steps. For to this you
have been called, because Christ also suffered for you,
leaving you an example, so that you might follow in his steps.*

1 PETER 2:13, 21

Week Six • Day Four

Ezra 8:21–36

We had practiced long and hard and were ready for a summer of traveling the highways throughout the United States to bring the hope of Jesus to many churches and youth camps. At least we thought we were ready—until tragedy struck. The night before our small band of college students was to leave, our equipment was stolen and destroyed. What we thought would be a day of readying for a celebration concert with our friends and family turned into a day of scurrying around the city attempting to replace our band and sound equipment.

We were able to replace everything and leave on time, but there was one thing that happened that day to correct our course, and I believe it made all the difference. Before we spent the day gathering new supplies, our leader had us sit among the destruction and pray. This time we spent together refocused our hearts and motives toward the reason God had called us on this summer journey. It was a defining moment on our team that set the stage for God to move not only in those who would hear our message, but in our lives too.

It appeared that Ezra was set to continue the journey to Jerusalem. He now had a small group of men who could assist him with the priestly tasks God had given him to accomplish, but there was still something that was preventing them from their travel.

Read Ezra 8:21–23.

» **What did Ezra ask the people to do at the river of Ahava?**

» **What was the purpose behind this action?**

» Why did he not feel he could ask the king for help in this area?

» How could this act, with the continuation of their journey, be a testimony to the king and people of the land?

Ezra demonstrated great faith as he trusted God to provide protection during their travel. Calling the people together for prayer and fasting would enable them to experience God's provision. Ezra could have gone into his tent and sought the Lord on his own with the same results, yet as the leader of these people, he recognized that his role was to direct them toward a life of worship. This involved including them in this practice.

Although they still had several months of travel before them, their participation in the request for safety strengthened their faith, and they were able to experience firsthand that God provided all they needed.

Our travelers still had a long way to go, but Ezra realized there were some means of protection he must take for their journey. I have a feeling that God revealed this to him during his time of prayer and fasting.

Read Ezra 8:24–30.

» **What did Ezra ask the priest to do?**

» **Why was this a task for the priest?**

» **What would have been Ezra's strategy within this process?**

Read Ezra 8:31–34.

» **What was the result of their prayer and fasting?**

» **How many days were they in Jerusalem before they began the next task before them? Why do you think they waited? (Think about what they had done and how they would be feeling.)**

Their journey was complete, and God's hand was evident along the way. When they arrived in Jerusalem, I honestly think they took a nap. They were exhausted and worn out! After a bit of rest, they brought the treasures to the temple and they prepared for sacrifice. They were now ready to reclaim their worship in the house of their God! What a blessed time this would be!

Unleash the Power of Praise:

Reclaim the blessing of God found as we worship Him alone.

Has there been a time in your life when you participated in fasting and prayer that resulted in your needs being met by the Almighty? How did this experience strengthen your faith? Have you used that experience to encourage others?

I have a dear friend who has shared with me her experiences of fasting with prayer. We're not talking just a day or two of fasting, but many, many weeks. In fact, she and her husband have done a forty-day fast twice. I remember that the first time I heard her story, I thought to myself, *How could anyone do that? She must be a su-*

per Christian with extraordinary faith. But the more I have gotten to know her, the more I see that she is just a woman who recognizes her brokenness. She knows her need for God to work in places where there seem to be no answers. Through her fasting, she found strength in her God when she was at her weakest. Her practice may not have resulted in the exact answer to her prayers she wanted, but I have seen something so much greater result in her. What emerged from this intense time of obedience is a woman who has faith to move mountains. No matter what God has allowed to come into her life, she meets each challenge with the certainty that God's hand is upon her—and that kind of faith is contagious!

She has been such a source of encouragement to me in this area of my life. I had never been in a practice of fasting, but the first time I felt God leading me to pray and fast, she was there to help me along the way. I remember her sitting on my sofa encouraging me through my questions and wonderings. She prayed with me and sent me Scripture throughout those few days to sustain me. Her faith has spurred me on to a life of obedience, especially in the area of prayer and fasting. God may not have answered my prayers in the way I have sought, or at least not yet, but He has given me so much more—a faith to trust Him knowing that His hand is upon me!

Ezra knew that involving the people in fasting and praying would strengthen them. As they saw God's blessing of protection, they knew He was answering their request. It was a life-changing experience that encouraged them in their faith long after they arrived in Jerusalem.

> *Four things let us ever keep in mind: God hears prayer, God heeds prayer,*
> *God answers prayer, and God delivers by prayer.*
> —E. M. Bounds

WEEK SIX • DAY FIVE

Reflection and Application

The people gathered! We ended yesterday with Ezra and the people arriving in Jerusalem. After a short rest they came together. Those who had arrived before gathered with those who had just made their way through the desert. I'm sure the celebration was joyous as stories were shared from their time apart.

Those who had been in Jerusalem would share both the difficulty and delight they had experienced while rebuilding the temple. Those who had just arrived may have given updates on friends and family still living in Babylon. But their primary goal was to worship together!

Read Ezra 8:35–36.

» **What was the first thing the people did when they gathered, and why was this significant at the end of their journey (v. 35)?**

» **What was the second thing the people did, and why was this significant to their arrival (v. 36)?**

» **Think back to chapter 7, specifically verses 25–26. What were the orders from the king that were needed as they continued life in the land of Judah?**

God's hand was upon them! He provided everything they needed. But the real work was just getting started. As they assimilated into their new homes, Ezra gathered the men needed for the next set of rebuilding. This rebuilding was not with brick and mortar, but was the rebuilding of lives and hearts.

He reminded the people of their position as the chosen people of God, along with their practices, as they lived according to the law. He guided them to reclaim the blessings that God had promised them as they realigned their hearts toward proper worship.

Unleash the Power of Praise:

Reflect on what God is teaching us personally about our worship.

We are chosen for so much more than the construction of buildings; we are chosen for building lives. This process begins with your own life. Recognizing who you are is crucial to carrying out God's plan for your life.

Be reminded today of who you are because of Jesus! Read through the Scripture below that we have discussed in detail, and recall how this applies to you.

Claim the truths and use your words to accept them as they are spoken over you. Be blessed through these promises. God is for you, and His hand is upon you!

> As you come to him, a living stone rejected by men
> but in the sight of God chosen and precious,
> you yourselves like living stones are being built up as a spiritual house,
> to be a holy priesthood,
> to offer spiritual sacrifices acceptable to God through Jesus Christ. . . .
> But you are a chosen race, a royal priesthood,
> a holy nation, a people for his own possession,
> that you may proclaim the excellencies of him who called you
> out of darkness into his marvelous light. (1 Peter 2:4–5, 9)

Be encouraged. God has called you! Oh, that we would be women who recognize

His calling on our lives and live each moment running toward it. There are so many blessings that await us as we live a life of worship to Him alone!

Just as Ezra was successful in the mission God had given him, we can find success. Why? Because the hand of the Lord is upon us!

There is nothing better for a person than that he should eat and drink and find enjoyment in his toil. This also, I saw, is from the hand of God, for apart from him who can eat or who can have enjoyment? For to the one who pleases him God has given wisdom and knowledge and joy.

ECCLESIASTES 2:24–26

REVIEW AND DISCUSSION

Day One

1. How have you seen the hand of the Lord upon your life?
2. What three characteristics do we see of Ezra in Ezra 7:10? Why would this be important to His calling?
3. Of these three actions, which are easy and which are a struggle? What can you do to be faithful in all three?

Day Two

1. What details would you love to find in the Scriptures that are not there?
2. How do we know that the decisions we make are in the will of God?

Day Three

1. Whether you are the leader or a participant, how important are the team members you have around you in ministry?
2. What does following Jesus cost you?

Day Four

1. Has there been a circumstance in your life when you stopped to pray, and it made all the difference?
2. Does that same prayer in community enhance the request? How?

Day Five

1. What truths do you claim of your identity in Christ because of what Jesus has done for you?
2. What is your takeaway for this week of study?

TEACHING NOTES

_____

_____

_____

_____

_____

_____

_____

_____

_____

_____

_____

_____

_____

_____

_____

_____

_____

_____

_____

_____

Repent

Week Seven

WEEK SEVEN • DAY ONE

Ezra 9:1–4

"And at the evening sacrifice, I rose from my fasting with my garment and my cloak torn, and fell upon my knees and spread out my hands to the Lord my God."
(Ezra 9:5)

More than one hundred years had passed since the first wave of exiles traveled back to the land of Judah. I wish I could tell you that all was well in the land where the rebuilt temple stood. Alas, that was not the case. In fact, the sins of the past generations, from as far back as the conquest of Joshua, were haunting the people. They just couldn't seem to live as the covenant people of God in the land He had so graciously given them—twice!

Ezra returned with a second group of exiles, including priests and temple servants. He had a very important role in this historical narrative, but found himself dealing with sin.

I want to warn you that this book does not seem to end well. The Bible is not a fairy tale where we close each epic drama with the words, "And they lived happily ever after." In fact, there are not many smiles in these last two chapters. Sin pervaded the hearts of the exiles, from the lowly citizen to those in positions of authority. It's a sin that has plagued God's people since the very beginning. But in their sin, we can still find hope.

When Moses led the Israelites out of Egypt to enter the promised land, God had some very strict instructions for them to follow. Let's journey back to the days when the promised land was still a promise.

Read Deuteronomy 7:1–5.

» **What were the instructions given to the Israelites as they entered the land?**

Take note of the seven nations that were to be destroyed.

» What were the instructions on marriage?

» What is the reason for this law?

Read Deuteronomy 7:6–8.

» Why did God choose the Israelites as His treasured possession?

Read Genesis 22:18.

» What will God do through His people that will benefit the entire world?

We know from our weeks in this study that God's people did not fully obey His commands. They did not take complete possession of the land, and they intermarried with the foreign nations. As a result of their disobedience, they have not yet seen the nations blessed. They were reminded of the consequences their ancestors endured, yet they still chose to go their way.

The exiles continued this pattern, struggling to follow the commands found in the law of Moses. Ezra had been in Jerusalem just over four months when the sin of the people was exposed.

Read Ezra 9:1–2.

» Who approached Ezra?

» What issue did they bring to him?

» Who of the exiles committed the greatest of sins?

» What was the characteristic labeled to those who had committed this sin?

» What does faithlessness look like? Why would this cause someone to sin?

I'm quite sure many people of the land attempted to justify their reasons for marrying among the foreign nations. Maybe there weren't enough women to go around, so they assumed it was better to marry and carry on the family name than to let their family die out. We read in Malachi 2:10-16 that some men even divorced their Jewish wives to marry foreigners. It could have been beauty, wealth, notoriety, or various other reasons that enticed them to intermarry.

Take note of the foreign nations in Ezra 9:1.

» What do you notice about the names listed in Ezra 9 and the names of the nations in Deuteronomy 7?

» How did Israel's disobedience in the conquest of the promised land affect the exiles?

Consequences! The disobedience of one generation will surely infect the next, just like germs that spread the flu. It was not just a problem in the ancient world, but it is one that is prevalent in our lives today! From the disobedience of a teenager to the fall of a church leader, the consequences affect us all. Some consequences are just mere inconveniences, such as a car taken away from a teenager and the parent now having to play taxi. But oftentimes, consequences have devastating results.

» Think of a time in your life when the consequences of someone else's sin affected you. You may not want to share the circumstance with others, but recall how you were able to move forward.

» Ezra recognized the seriousness of the sin that was brought to the surface. He knew that if this sin was not dealt with, it could destroy everything that the people had accomplished upon their return.

» What role was Ezra given by the king according to the letter that he had written, found in Ezra 7:25–26?

» What would be the consequence for disobedience to God's law?

Read Ezra 9:3–4.

» What was Ezra's response?

» Who else responded?

» How would you describe the reaction of someone who is appalled by sin?

» How would you describe the general reaction to sin in our world?

Ezra did not immediately begin to cast down judgment on the people who committed this sin. Instead, we find him grieving this sin before God and joined by some of the people who trembled along with him. Not everyone joined Ezra before the Lord—only those who recognized the gravity of what had been done.

Unleash the Power of Praise:

Rediscover the meaning of worship.

Even in ancient times, sin did not make all people tremble. Our world today falls into the same trap, as sin is often celebrated and portrayed as entertainment. This is one of the roadblocks we encounter as we attempt to bring the truth of the gospel into our broken world.

People need a Savior, yet they do not recognize their need for salvation. What do they need to be saved from if they do not see their current state as sinful?

The "If it feels good, do it" mentality gives little credence to a conviction of sin. The biblical definition of sin is no longer recognized as valid to those who have made themselves the god of their own selves. Their worship is completely focused on self and not on the Savior.

Think of how this is true in your circle of influence. How can you reach a sin-filled world that does not acknowledge they are sinners?

Read Ephesians 4:17–25. Use this as a guide to pray for those in your world who do not know God and do not recognize their sin.

Recall the mindset of the one who does not know God.

Reflect on the state of the believer who is in Christ.

Respond to the call that is placed on your life to love those who need a Savior.

This is your worship!

> Now this I say and testify in the Lord, that you must no longer walk as the Gentiles do, in the futility of their minds. They are darkened in their understanding, alienated from the life of God because of the ignorance that is in them, due to their hardness of heart. They have become callous and have given themselves up to sensuality, greedy to practice every kind of impurity. But that is not the way you learned Christ!—assuming that you have heard about him and were taught in him, as the truth is in Jesus, to put off your old self, which belongs to your former manner of life and is corrupt through deceitful desires, and to be renewed in the spirit of your minds, and to put on the new self, created after the likeness of God in true righteousness and holiness. Therefore, having put away falsehood, let each one of you speak the truth with his neighbor, for we are members one of another. (Ephesians 4:17–25)

Christ is never fully valued until sin is clearly seen. We must know the depth and malignity of our disease in order to appreciate the great Physician.

—J. C. RYLE

WEEK SEVEN • DAY TWO

Ezra 9:6–15

Every sin is rooted in something we don't believe about God.
—TIM KELLER

When you're in love with someone, your demonstration of that love is delightful to them. Your engagement shows love as you provide for them in everyday acts of service.

I am blessed to be married to a man whose love is demonstrated toward me daily. Each morning he makes sure my coffee cup is always filled. When I leave for the office, he always walks me to the door. At times when life is so busy and I can barely keep my head above water, he takes over the household duties I often do. There is no doubt in my mind that he knows me and my needs at any moment. His acts of service display the vastness of his love for me.

The same is true about our God as we respond to Him in our lives. The more we know about Him, the more deeply we fall in love with Him, which results in our service to Him becoming our greatest joy.

Spending time in God's Word leads us to know our God personally. The Bible is our resource to learn about God's character, which is immutable—never changing. When we comprehend the nature of God and realize His love for us, we live in a place of complete recognition of our value. Although we have no worth on our own, our worth comes from the blood of Jesus, and because of Him, we are declared righteous before our King!

The opposite is true as well. When we find ourselves looking for value in something other than God, our lives take a turn for the worst. Believing that God is not sufficient for our everyday needs will propel us toward worldly pleasures to fill the void that is within our hearts. We then may have feelings of worthlessness and see ourselves as helpless in our circumstances. Our truth of who God is becomes diminished, and we find ourselves spiraling deep into a pit of sin, not sure how we will ever escape, and often, not wanting to be rescued.

The people in Ezra's day fell into grievous sin. They forgot that God is faithful and that

He would provide them the spouses they needed in order to continue their family lines. Their actions demonstrated hearts that perhaps believed in God, but did not believe God. They failed to recognize that He was sufficient for all their needs. God's laws were not written to bring them into bondage, but to bring them into their very best life. They neglected to embrace God's great love for them and all that He had brought them through.

In Ezra 9 we find Ezra before the Lord, crying out for the people. Even though Ezra was innocent of their transgressions, he came before God identifying himself with the people.

As you read through each portion of Ezra's prayer, circle every time there is a plural pronoun (we, our, us, etc.).

Read Ezra 9:6–9.

» **What images did Ezra use to describe the seriousness of their sin (v. 6)?**

» **What comparison did Ezra give to describe their sin (v. 7)?**

» **God demonstrates his grace (favor) on the people. What were the four ways grace was shown (v. 8)?**

   » 1. Leave us a _____.

   » 2. Give us a _____ _____ within His holy place.

   » 3. _____ our eyes.

   » 4. Grant us a little _____ in our _____.

» **Think back over the story of the exiles. Give an example of each way God showed favor upon His people as they attested to His provision in verse 9.**

   » **God has not forsaken us in our slavery:**

» God extended His steadfast love before the kings of Persia:

» God gave us protection:

Read Ezra 9:10–15.

» Ezra was speechless because the law given to the people had been defiled. Write out the portion of this passage that cites the law they defiled.

» Why did Ezra express that this time the law broken was worse than the other times Israel defiled the commands of God (vv. 13–14)?

» What was the posture of Ezra and the people as they recognized their guilt in this matter (v. 15)?

» What characteristic of God led them to this place (v. 15)?

» What does it mean that God is just?

Read 1 John 1:9.

» How would you describe the faithfulness and justice of God in the act of repentance?

Unleash the Power of Praise:

Realize the challenges found in the misalignment of our worship of God.

The posture of our worship is critical to the placement of our heart before our God. There is a beauty that is found in humble submission when we are found bending low before our God. Recognition of His perfect character produces reverent fear, bringing us to worship on our knees.

There will come a day when "at the name of Jesus every knee should bow, in heaven and on earth and under the earth" (Philippians 2:10). But until that day when the whole world bows on bended knee, we believers can find great pleasure as we choose this posture. Why? Because we have the choice to bow on bended knee. This choice is met with the heart of a Christ follower who recognizes that her King is worthy of her worship.

Take a moment to read the account of Simon Peter as he was found bowing his knee before the Messiah.

Read the account in Luke 5:1–11.

What did Jesus do that Simon was not able to do on his own (vv. 5–6)?

What was Simon's reaction (v. 8)?

Why did Simon react this way (v. 9)?

What did Jesus tell them that would change their lives forever (v. 10)?

How did Simon and the other fishermen respond to Jesus (v. 11)?

After three years of following Jesus, the disciples fell back into their former lives.

Read John 21:3–7. Remember that they have witnessed the death and resurrection of Jesus at this point in the narrative.

What was the similar circumstance they found themselves in, and what did Jesus do for them?

What was Simon's reaction?

Simon Peter's reaction to Jesus's provision appears similar in John 21, yet the motivation was different. The first time Simon reacted, it was out of fear. He had an encounter with God that made him tremble. He was unworthy, yet Jesus called him to follow. The second time he recognized Jesus as Lord—well, after John's observation—and swam toward the Savior he knew and loved.

Peter had come full circle, from fear to faith. He had found the blessed freedom we have when we know our God. It is a freedom that comes only from experiencing God's perfect love. "Perfect love casts out fear" (1 John 4:18).

This is true for us as well. We come to a place where our posture before our God in our confession is transformed because we have found Him to be faithful and we recognize He is just, culminating in the blessed truth that He will forgive.

Do you have an example in your own life that has led you from fear to faith in your daily worship of God?

Is there a circumstance that currently has you stuck in fear?

As I write this morning, a dear friend is dropping her husband off for a very serious surgery on his colon. The pandemic in our world has forced our hospitals to close its doors to visitors and family members, so she must wait for the results at home. As we talked this morning, I see a woman with a faith that is steadfast and strong, but it wasn't always this way. There was a time when she'd encounter difficulty and would fall apart in fear of what would happen next, oftentimes due to the sin of another far out of her control.

Even though this surgery is not a result of sin, it has ushered her once again into the unknown. But this time, her *what if* questions are met with a peace that only God can bring.

Her cry contained these words: "My mind is set upon Him as I gaze upon Jesus. We serve a mighty God."

She has not fallen to the ground in fear of what may happen, but in awe of her God. She knows Him well, and the worship of her life is evident.

May we fall before our God today in complete dependence. If there are circumstances plaguing your soul today due to the sin of another or a situation beyond your control, come before Him in your worship. God already knows, and He is longing to show Himself faithful!

I can rest in the fact that God is in control, which means I can face things that are out of my control and not act out of control.
—Lysa TerKeurst

WEEK SEVEN • DAY THREE

Ezra 10:1–17

As we read the last chapter in the book of Ezra, we find a people ready to face the consequences of their sin. Their response did not come from an emotional hype that rallied everyone toward confession. Their response came because one man prayed!

» Can there be danger found in an emotional response that is created by hype toward the things of God? If yes, how would you describe the danger?

» How does real revival take place in the life of God's people and within the church? Read Psalm 51:17.

James 5:16 tell us, "Therefore, confess your sins to one another and pray for one another, that you may be healed. The prayer of a righteous person has great power as it is working." Ezra had spent time praying for the people, and God began to move.
Read Ezra 10:1–8.

» What happened while Ezra prayed (v. 1)?

» Who stepped forward as a spokesperson for the people (v. 2)?

» Even though the people had "broken faith" with God, what encouragement did Shecaniah bring to Ezra (v. 2)?

» What were the two actions found in the covenant that Shecaniah proposed (v. 3)?

» Ezra agreed with the covenant, but before he began the task to establish it, what action did he take (v. 6)?

» What does this tell you about Ezra's thoughts on dealing with the people's sin?

A proclamation was made, and the people of Judah had three days to travel to Jerusalem. The stakes were high, for if they did not show up, they would be disowned by their people and their land would be taken away. This consequence, no doubt, motivated the people to pack their things and head quickly to the city. I'm sure many of them wondered why they were being called together on such short notice. Had they heard of Ezra's discovery of the law they had broken? Were they were completely oblivious to the reason they were called to gather? Whatever the case, they came, and three days later they all sat in the pouring rain, trembling over their sin!

Read Ezra 10:9–17.

» Summarize the message Ezra gave to the people.

» What was the response of the people to his words (v. 12)?

» What was the excuse the people gave for not wanting to stay in the city (v. 13)?

The people were ready to come before the spiritual leaders, but they didn't want to stand in the rain. We find that this process took four months, and so even though it sounds like a bunch of whining, I can see their dilemma.

The people were called before the council one by one to find if their marriage was ordained within the law of God. Those who were found innocent would return home, but those who were guilty would be called to action. True repentance requires action and admitting the truth of what has been done. Repentance isn't just being sorry for the sin that was committed. Often when we are found in sin, our sorrow arises because we've been caught. Repentance requires a change. The people in our narrative have to do something about the problem of intermarriage. It wasn't enough to just be sorry.

The change that had to be made was uncomfortable and hard. Remember that the people we read about in Scripture are humans with real emotions. When the text tells us they trembled, we should feel that weight in our soul, knowing that what was going to be asked of them would cause much heartache.

The task before them was not easy, but in order for them to worship God alone, they had to make a change. True worship begins with repentance.

Unleash the Power of Praise:

Recognize the truths found in God's Word that encourage us to worship.

In the account of the woman at the well, we find that the direction of her worship is challenged by truth—the truth not only about worship, but also about her current sinful state.

Jesus confronted this woman in her sin of multiple marriages and living with a man to whom she was not married. She attempted to derail the conversation and spoke about worshiping God to give the appearance of a heart aligned to right worship. But the all-knowing Jesus did not allow her to hinder the real work that needed to be done in her life—the work of repentance.

Jesus affirms that the focus of worship is of the utmost importance, but it begins with truth: "But the hour is coming, and is now here, when the true worshipers will worship the Father in spirit and truth, for the Father is seeking such people to worship him" (John 4:23).

When she acknowledged the truth of her circumstances, her repentance would lead her into all truth, and that truth would realign her worship—a change that is hard, but a change that would bring others into repentance to find the truth that Jesus had to offer! He was the truth they were looking for!

When I think about my sin, I discover it is usually deep within my heart, unknown to the world around me. It is often found in pride and silent judgments of others. It is more about my lack of response to the promptings of the Spirit as He beckons me to reach out and help or share the gospel. It is found in my fears of saying yes to something that may cause me to be rejected or even to give up precious time.

What about you? Is there something in your own life that you have been pushing to the side, hoping that no one would notice? Is there something God has been asking you to do that you find excuses to dismiss?

Meditate on Psalm 32 and discover the progression of the psalmist as he acknowledges his sin to the Almighty and rejoices in His forgiveness. As you do, write beside each portion your own prayer as it follows the archetype of this petition.

Blessed is the one   **Promise**

whose transgressions are forgiven,
whose sins are covered.
Blessed is the one
whose sin the Lord does not count against them
and in whose spirit is no deceit.

When I kept silent,   Admission
my bones wasted away
through my groaning all day long.
For day and night
your hand was heavy on me;
my strength was sapped
as in the heat of summer.

Then I acknowledged my sin to you   Confession
and did not cover up my iniquity.
I said, "I will confess
my transgressions to the Lord."
And you forgave
the guilt of my sin.

Therefore let all the faithful pray to you   Thanksgiving
while you may be found;
surely the rising of the mighty waters
will not reach them.
You are my hiding place;
you will protect me from trouble
and surround me with songs of deliverance.

I will instruct you and teach you   Wisdom
in the way you should go;
I will counsel you with my loving eye on you.
Do not be like the horse or the mule,
which have no understanding
but must be controlled by bit and bridle
or they will not come to you.

**Many are the woes of the wicked,
but the Lord's unfailing love
surrounds the one who trusts in him.**

**Rejoice in the Lord and be glad, you righteous;   Praise
sing, all you who are upright in heart! (Psalm 32 NIV)**

Acknowledging our sin and bringing it before our God cannot be something that is forced. This act must come from a heart that is willing. Maybe today is not the day you are ready to confront a specific sin in your life. You know deep down that you have asked God to forgive, but then you find yourself doing it again and again.

This is not uncommon, for I have found myself in the same place, and still do at times. But this I know—not only is God faithful and just to forgive, but He will also give us the ability to resist the temptation when it comes, as 1 John tell us.

The author of Hebrews encourages us: "For we do not have a high priest who is unable to sympathize with our weaknesses, but one who in every respect has been tempted as we are, yet without sin. Let us then with confidence draw near to the throne of grace, that we may receive mercy and find grace to help in time of need" (Hebrews 4:15–16).

We can come before His throne in confidence, knowing that His grace and His mercy will be extended to us in our sin and when temptation is before us. Take courage, daughter of the King—He can handle your sin. Bringing it before Him is an act of worship.

*The nearer a man lives to God, the more intensely
has he to mourn over his own evil heart.*
—Charles H. Spurgeon

Week Seven • Day Four

Ezra 10:18–44

We have arrived! We have reached the last words of the book of Ezra. Within this chapter lies a very abrupt ending to the story of the returned exiles. But this postexilic saga is not over, for the book of Nehemiah continues the story.

When first written, these two books were considered one. There is much debate over the authorship of these books. Some believe the person who wrote 1 and 2 Chronicles was the unknown author of Ezra. Others believe it was Ezra himself, as the latter part of the book that bears his name is written in first person. Regardless of the author, the conclusion of the book is our study for today.

As you read through this portion, you may want to play it from an audible Bible. The names are many and are difficult to pronounce. Nonetheless, it is the work of our reading, so let's get to it!

Read Ezra 10:18–44.

The passage tells us there are more than one hundred men who were found guilty of the sin of intermarriage. This list includes twenty-seven priests and temple servants. When leadership is found to be in a lifestyle of sin, the people will certainly follow.

This number is relatively low compared to the number of exiles who returned to Jerusalem. Fifty thousand strong arrived more than one hundred years ago, and their numbers were sure to have increased. Less than one percent of the people were found guilty of sin, but the leaders recognized its severity. Dealing with these transgressions while they were small would rescue the nation from complete destruction.

These were the men who were asked to repent and do something very difficult. The marriages to their foreign wives would be annulled, and the women, along with their children, would be sent back to their foreign lands. That may seem harsh to us, and I'm quite certain the process brought anguish and tears, as women had to leave the men they loved and children were taken away from the only father they had ever known. But the leaders were following the pattern that had been practiced by their people long before the exile.

Read Genesis 21:9–14.

» **How did Abraham first respond to Sarah's request about sending Hagar and Ishmael away?**

» **What instructions did God give to Abraham?**

» **What promise did God remind Abraham of that He would accomplish through Isaac?**

» **What gracious promise was given to Ishmael?**

» **What could have been the repercussions to the promise if Hagar and Ishmael stayed with Abraham?**

We may not understand the reasoning behind these circumstances and may wrestle with the thought of abandoning women and children. I hope you do, because it sounds awful in our humanness!

What we do know is this drastic time called for drastic measures. The people of God had been given strict laws to protect the purity of the people. It wasn't because God did not love those outside of His chosen people; we know that it was His plan all along to bless the nations. But God knew that the hearts of His people would be bent toward the gods of the world, and

He put a means of protection in place to preserve His people—a people whose lineage would birth His very Son.

I have always been struck by the tragic way the book of Ezra ends. This list at the end of the book is a list of people who broke God's law. It includes many destroyed lives and families torn apart by sin. But as I read through this list again to write this study, God gave me a new perspective on the people found in this story's ending.

Our book of Ezra began with a long list of people who returned. They were the people who believed God enough to travel a difficult road and arrive in a place of destruction. After many years of opposition and trials, the work they had set out to accomplish was complete. Their worship was renewed as they were reacquainted with their God.

The book of Ezra ends with another list. They were a people who believed God enough to travel the difficult road of repentance. They were willing to do the real work needed to experience true confession, regardless of the consequences. They would no doubt face opposition and trials as they moved forward, making the changes that were asked of them. And in the end, they would find redemption. They would become a redeemed people because they turned from their sin and found that their God was trustworthy. It was in their God they would place their hope.

Unleash the Power of Praise:

Reclaim the blessing of God found as we worship Him alone.

Shecaniah saw hope for Israel even before their confession began: "We have broken faith with our God and have married foreign women from the peoples of the land, but even now there is hope for Israel in spite of this" (Ezra 10:2). It was seen in the blessed act of atonement.

Sacrifices were made for each person on the list, and the blood from those sacrifices would cover their sins and leave them clean. "For the life of the flesh is in the blood, and I have given it for you on the altar to make atonement for your souls, for it is the blood that makes atonement by the life" (Leviticus 17:11).

Although the blood of many animals would be shed to cover a multitude of sin in the years to come, the atonement would be accomplished once and for all on the cross. When Jesus shed His blood, it cleansed the sins of all those who believe in Him.

John is writing to believers in 1 John 2:1–2 as he says, "My little children, I am writing these things to you so that you may not sin. But if anyone does sin, we have an advocate with the Father, Jesus Christ the righteous. He is the propitiation [atonement] for our sins, and not for ours only but also for the sins of the whole world."

When we take a second glance at the names found at the end of this book, we see the glorious grace of God demonstrated to those who have sinned. According to the law, they have become restored unto God. This is the blessed hope we have as believers.

We are a people who are born dead in our sins. "But God, being rich in mercy, because of the great love with which he loved us, even when we were dead in our trespasses, made us alive together with Christ—by grace you have been saved—and raised us up with him and seated us with him in the heavenly places in Christ Jesus, so that in the coming ages he might show the immeasurable riches of his grace in kindness toward us in Christ Jesus" (Ephesians 2:4–7).

This is the gospel, and the blessed truth found within gives cause to worship!

Take a moment and worship God by thanking Him
- **for your salvation**
- **for His mercy and grace**
- **for our position in the heavenlies**
- **for Jesus!**

It is the gospel that leads us to daily rebuild our life of worship. His sacrifice propels us to live our lives for Him alone. If you have not come to a place where you have trusted in Jesus, the time is now! God provided a way for you to no longer be a slave to sin, but to live victorious in Christ.

Salvation comes from no one else but Jesus. If you are ready to believe in Him, acknowledge three things today:

First, admit to God you are aware that you are a sinner and you need a Savior.

Romans 3:23–25 says, "For all have sinned and fall short of the glory of God, and are justified by his grace as a gift, through the redemption that is in Christ Jesus, whom God put forward as a propitiation by his blood, to be received by faith. This was to show God's righteousness, because in his divine forbearance he had passed over former sins."

Then acknowledge what Jesus accomplished on the cross through His shed blood, the atonement for your sins. This is a free gift offered to anyone who will believe.

Romans 6:23 tells us, "For the wages of sin is death, but the free gift of God is eternal life in Christ Jesus our Lord."

Last, proclaim that Jesus is your Savior. Find your hope in Him alone, and accept His grace and mercy.

> If you confess with your mouth that Jesus is Lord and believe in your heart that God raised him from the dead, you will be saved. For with the heart one believes and is justified, and with the mouth one confesses and is saved. For the Scripture says, "Everyone who believes in him will not be put to shame." For there is no distinction between Jew and Greek; for the same Lord is Lord of all, bestowing his riches on all who call on him. For "everyone who calls on the name of the Lord will be saved." (Romans 10:9–13)

If you made this decision today, the angels of heaven are rejoicing, and so am I. Now tell someone! Then, if you do not already attend a place that teaches this truth, find a church so you can begin to grow in your faith. I would love to know of your decision, and you can contact me at carollynntetzlaff@gmail.com.

Today your life has been changed for eternity, and that is reason to worship!

WEEK SEVEN • DAY FIVE

Reflection and Application

God created us to be worshipers. If it is not God who resides at the center of our worship, something else will take His place because we must worship.

The narrative of the exiles' return to Jerusalem has taken us on a journey from broken to beautiful, filled with both misplaced and magnificent worship. We watched them succumb to opposition of the enemy and fall into sins of their fleshly desires. But we also saw them rebuild the temple, reestablish their worship, and return from their sin through repentance.

During our time in Ezra, we have been challenged—like the exiles—to realign our hearts to worship God alone. Worship is not an event that takes place; worship is a lifestyle that seeks to glorify God in every thought, word, and deed.

This last week in Ezra brought about the need for repentance in our lives. Repentance brings about real-life change that is necessary to live out our worship of God.

Remember back to Ezra 4 when the exiles got distracted and stopped building the temple? They spent sixteen years focusing on their own kingdoms, leaving the temple and their worship in a state of rubble. Our conversation turned to the things in our own lives that distract us, but today we need to get a little deeper.

Our worship is hindered by distractions, and sometimes those distractions can become sin. Sin can slip into our lives and leave us unaware of the division it has placed between us and our God.

The struggle to get my zipper down on the back of my dress caused me to rip the seam in frustration. As the fabric gave way, the taffeta garment fell to the floor along with my tears. It was late, and I was exhausted. The excitement and busyness of the past few days had been the perfect mask for my pain. I had been part of a stunning occasion, culminating in the union of two very good friends.

I really was happy for them. But as I ended the night alone, standing in my closet with tear-stained cheeks, my only thought was, *Why not me?*

Familiar thoughts plagued my mind as I cried out in an audible voice, not even caring if anyone heard. *What am I doing wrong? Am I not serving enough, reading my Bible enough, praying enough? What is it that I need to do?*

Feeling quite alone that night, a shift took place in my life that left me completely unaware of the change. I began to live a double life of having the appearance of pleasing God at church, yet engaging in friendships that were less than edifying.

Longing to be married caused me to spend time with a man who was far from Christ; in fact, he was an atheist. Although romance was not part of our future, his friendship drew me further and further from what I knew to be right, all the while continuing to serve my local church behind my mask.

The secrets I kept deep inside were disguised by doing the right thing, albeit with the wrong motives. My worship had shifted. Instead of being a sold-out follower of Jesus, I moved toward the relationships and activities that brought me emotional happiness. Even though this time brought much laughter and fun, the Holy Spirit never allowed me to have peace.

This short season of my life ended abruptly one night as I lay in bed after an evening out with my friends. Unable to sleep, I felt a pull within my soul, as if there were a game of tug-of-war taking place. The Spirit's promptings were so strong that I began to weep. The double life I had been living was about to end.

It was that night that I cried and prayed like never before. I was done with this facade, and I brought all my sins before God's throne. At first, I was filled with much shame and didn't want to utter the words, but the Spirit reminded me that He already knew and that His love for me had not changed. It wasn't enough to simply ask for His forgiveness, at least not for me; I needed to do something drastic to assure myself that I was serious in the moment of repentance. It was all or nothing.

My prayer ended with a sincere pledge to my King. I made a promise to realign my worship to serve God alone in every aspect of my life, including my relationships. This commitment included a vow not to date anyone for five years, a very courageous move for a girl who had just turned twenty-nine.

The next morning when I woke up, I felt free for the first time in years. John 10:10 suddenly had new meaning for me: "I came that [you] may have life and have it abundantly." The fullness of life had returned to my soul, and I began to live in the joy only God can give.

The next five years tells a story of its own, but this next season brought me to a place where the service of my King was all I desired. The blessings that came on this journey were bountiful, my time with Him was sweet, and surprisingly, the time passed quickly. The five years ended with a new friendship, which in time would blossom into the life I now live with my adoring husband. He truly is my "Happily ever after!"

I am so very grateful that the hidden sin of my life was exposed within my soul and a life of proper worship was rekindled.

When our worship becomes misaligned, we can become blinded to what should be obvious. Gossip, lying, cheating, stealing, etc. can be blaring signs of our disobedience. Other times, our sin is so deeply rooted that it takes the work of the Spirit to reveal to us things that are typically hidden from the surface of our lives.

These sins are the ones from which all the outward iniquities will eventually flow. Ephesians 4:31 (NLT) tells us to get rid of them: "Get rid of all bitterness, rage, anger, harsh words, and slander, as well as all types of evil behavior." These actions are the very root of the sin found on the surface of our lives. They are the attitudes of the heart, which means it's the heart that must be transformed as we deal with sin. That's why Solomon wrote, "Guard your heart above all else, for it determines the course of your life" (Proverbs 4:23 NLT).

As we end this study, let's do some real heart work. Maybe you know your sin. Maybe it's obvious to you and even to those around you. But maybe you have to sit still and let the Spirit speak to you in the quiet. The more we know God, the more sin is detestable to us. We stay away from it because we know how much it hurts our heavenly Father. But the truth is, we still sin. It could be a fleeting thought or a harsh word. Maybe it's found in our faithlessness or our lack of believing that God is who He says He is.

» Reflect on the Scripture below and allow the Spirit to speak to you. Write down what He reveals.

Search me, O God, and know my heart;
test me and know my anxious thoughts.
Point out anything in me that offends you,
and lead me along the path of everlasting life. (Psalm 139:23–24 NLT)

» Take what has been revealed and confess it to God. Use the prayer of David from Psalm 51 as you launch into your own words of repentance.

Have mercy on me, O God,
according to your steadfast love;

according to your abundant mercy

blot out my transgressions.

Wash me thoroughly from my iniquity,

and cleanse me from my sin!

Behold, you delight in truth in the inward being,

and you teach me wisdom in the secret heart.

Purge me with hyssop, and I shall be clean;

wash me, and I shall be whiter than snow.

Let me hear joy and gladness;

let the bones that you have broken rejoice.

Hide your face from my sins,

and blot out all my iniquities.

Create in me a clean heart, O God,

and renew a right spirit within me.

Cast me not away from your presence,

and take not your Holy Spirit from me.

Restore to me the joy of your salvation,

and uphold me with a willing spirit.

For you will not delight in sacrifice, or I would give it;

you will not be pleased with a burnt offering.

The sacrifices of God are a broken spirit;

a broken and contrite heart, O God, you will not despise. (Psalm 51:1-2, 6-12,

16-17)

As we lay our sins at the feet of Jesus, we know that "He is faithful and just to forgive." He no longer remembers them, and we are made clean because of His atoning sacrifice. That leads me to worship! I hope you feel that way too.

My soul began singing the words to this song as I rejoice in the forgiveness of my own sins:

"Nothing but the Blood of Jesus"
Oh! precious is the flow
that makes me white as snow;
No other fount I know
Nothing but the blood of Jesus.

We are daughters of the King, adopted into His family because of His great love that saved us and keeps on saving us!

Unleash the Power of Praise:
Reflect on what God is teaching us personally about our worship.

Closing this book is like saying goodbye to a dear friend, or in this case, many friends. The exiles, along with their leaders—Joshua and Zerubbabel, the prophet Haggai, and Ezra the priest—have met with us each day. They have taught us what it looks like to be a worshiper of the Lord Most High.

They have helped us rediscover the meaning of worship as they traveled nine hundred miles to do the one thing God has asked. They recognized that worship wasn't just about the work of rebuilding, but was also about the daily offering of their lives in obedience.

What have you rediscovered about worship? Has your view of worship shifted since you began? Write a definition of worship that will guide you into a life that aligns with the heart of the Father.

These characters found in Ezra called us to realize the challenges found in the misalignment of our worship of God. Their discouragement caused them to turn away from their calling and turn to selfish desires. They chose what was easy over what was good, and they found themselves lacking in every way. The encouragement to return to their work realigned their hearts toward proper worship, and they began to find success.

What are the challenges you may face as you align your heart to worship God alone? What gets in the way of setting your heart on Him alone in every aspect of life?

In your family?

In your work?

In your ministry?

In your longings?

Once again, they recognized the truth found in God's words that encouraged them in their worship. Their identity was found in God alone, so when opposition came, they remembered God's promise to them: "We are the servants of the God of heaven and earth, and we are rebuilding" (Ezra 5:11).

What passages of Scripture of God's promises will you remember to rest in when life becomes challenging? How will you keep these verses in front of you?

What verses do you need to memorize?

What verses do you need to have written down and in your view?

How will you make time in the Word a priority in your life?

They reclaimed the blessing of God as they worshiped Him alone, rejoicing together in the finished work. This work would allow them to worship corporately as they gathered in the temple courtyard. It was a blessing that would be passed on for generations to come.

How will you maintain the practice of both personal and corporate worship in your life?

What blessings have you experienced in the past as you've chosen to worship God alone?

Finally, they reflected on what God was teaching them personally about their worship. As they were confronted with the gravity of their sin, they knew the resolution needed would bring much pain and sorrow to their families and friends. But as they turned and repented, their nation was blessed and they, once again, found joy in worshiping God alone.

After the time in this study and reflection on the truths you have discovered, what is a truth you can hold to as you close this book?

With whom can you share this truth? Ask them to hold you accountable for what God has revealed to you as you live a daily life of worship before Him.

I pray that your time in this book has brought you to a greater understanding of worship and into a vibrant life as a worshiper.

As I edited this last week of study, I asked this question to a dear author friend of mine: "Do you ever reread your study and come to the place where the words you wrote convict your own soul again and again?"

The book of Ezra continues to weave God's truth into every crevasse of my heart. It brings me to a place where I have to reevaluate the object of my worship each and every day. I don't ever want to forget what God showed me. I don't ever want to go back to the time when my worship was placed in anyone or anything other than the Almighty. The book of Ezra has worked in my innermost being to help me recognize those times when my eyes turn to focus on my own glory. The truths I learned have given me the blessed freedom to stop myself and repent. My desire is to live the abundant life God has promised, with my gaze fixed upon the Almighty and bringing glory to Him alone.

As you close this book, my prayer is that you find yourself to be a woman who is mindful of her worship—a woman who will daily live out Paul's words: "[I urge you, daughters of the King], by the mercies of God, to present your bodies as a living sacrifice, holy and acceptable to God, which is your spiritual worship. Do not be conformed to this world, but be transformed by the renewal of your mind, that by testing you may discern what is the will of God, what is good and acceptable and perfect" (Romans 12:1–2).

Dear friend, we are women of God, and we are rebuilding our lives of worship. May your life unleash the power of praise as you continue to daily rebuild your brokenness to beautiful through worship.

I would love to hear what God has done in your life during this time in His Word. I pray God has moved in your heart in such a way that you will never be the same. May the story of your life be found as worship in His eyes! He is worthy of your life of worship.

Please find me on my website at caroltetzlaff.com and share with me your story. May God bless you for your diligent study of His Word as you live your life in worship of your King.

REVIEW AND DISCUSSION

Day One

1. How does the disobedience of one generation affect the next? Have you seen this in your own life or in that of your family?
2. What is the response of sin in our world? How should a believer respond to sin?

Day Two

1. How is love demonstrated to you through a spouse, friend, or family member? How do you demonstrate love to others? How do you demonstrate love to God?
2. What is the difference between believing in God and believing God?

Day Three

1. Repentance isn't just being sorry for your sin. What else must occur for true repentance?
2. What are the promises God has for us as we find ourselves in sin?

Day Four

1. Even though less than one percent of the people were found in sin, why was it so important to lead them to a place of repentance before God and make things right?
2. Why was the consequence of this sin important to the purity of God's people?
3. What hope can you find in the ending of the book of Ezra?

Day Five

1. What is your takeaway from this week of study?
2. During this time in Ezra, how has your life been taken from broken to beautiful through worship?

TEACHING NOTES

_____

_____

_____

_____

_____

_____

_____

_____

_____

_____

_____

_____

_____

_____

_____

_____

_____

_____

_____

_____

ENDNOTES

[1] C. L. Feinberg, "Jeremiah," in *The Expositor's Bible Commentary: Isaiah, Jeremiah, Lamentations, Ezekiel*, ed. F. E. Gaebelein (Grand Rapids: Zondervan Publishing House, 1986), vol. 6, 551.

[2] *The Expositor's Bible Commentary: 1 & 2 Kings, 1 & 2 Chronicles, Ezra, Nehemiah, Esther, Job* (Grand Rapids: Zondervan Publishing House, 1986), vol. 4, 626.

[3] E. Yamauchi, "Ezra-Nehemiah," in *The Expositor's Bible Commentary: 1 & 2 Kings, 1 & 2 Chronicles, Ezra, Nehemiah, Esther, Job*, ed. F. E. Gaebelein (Grand Rapids: Zondervan Publishing House, 1986), vol 4., 633.

[4] www.olivetree.com/blog/what-does-it-mean-to-fear-the-lord.

[5] ESV Study Bible (Wheaton, IL: Crossway, 2001), 1,744.

[6] Mark I. Bubeck, *Warfare Praying* (Chicago: Moody Publishers, 2016), 100.

[7] https://www.jpost.com/middle-east/iran-news/iran-bulldozes-grave-of-christian-pastor-hanged-by-regime-614259.

ORDER INFORMATION

CPSIA information can be obtained
at www.ICGtesting.com
Printed in the USA
LVHW061101240521
688313LV00017B/1478